Images of Me

By

Dr. Jody Dempsey

ISBN: 1-4033-1245-1 (e-book)
ISBN: 1-4033-1246-X (Paperback)

This book is printed on acid free paper.

1stBooks - rev. 06/24/02

PREFACE

Life is really confusing. It has been right from the start. I mean, at some point you realize that you <u>are,</u> you recognize that you exist, that you're not alone, that you're a part of a larger reality. However, figuring out what that reality means and how you figure into it is another story altogether.

When I was a little girl, it didn't take a whole lot. The questions were fairly simple, like "Where's Mom and Dad?", "What's for dinner?", "Can I go out and play?", "Can Sara come over?" and so on. Obviously, not very deep stuff, and the answers weren't too complicated. ("At work," "Chicken and baked potatoes," "No, Molly, not now.") I don't recall having much difficulty then. However, lately it's been a whole different story. Sixteen seems much more confusing than six. That which was black and white, cut and dried, clear as the nose on your face, blah, blah, blah, is now gray, muddy, murky, and confusing as hell. And it hurts in places where it never hurt before, and with feelings I never felt.

The worst part is that I don't know if it's me, my parents, school, my friends, or some perverse combination of the whole bunch that has me so lost that I felt like I don't know a thing about myself, my world, or my place in it. All I see are images - illusions - ghosts - that float and flutter about me whispering so many conflicting messages. Images that at some points seem pretty good. You know, <u>reasonable</u>. However, just when you feel you may have something, you turn your head just a bit, gaze at it from a slightly different angle, hold it up to the sun to shine a sliver of light on it and just when you really, really need it, it's gone. What it means, who you are, who everybody else is, and where you're going. Poof! Disappeared! The whole thing! What's left is another image, no clearer than the last one, just as smoky, just as devoid of direction and meaning, just as suspect, just as likely to set me up for hurt and heartache as the last one.

But what are my choices? I used to feel I had a million of those but it seems that the older I get, the fewer I have. When you're little, you dream about the future when you'll be a "big girl," when you, too, can stay up late and wear make-up. Now I need cosmetics to cover the blemishes on my heart and soul. I haven't been able to find that in Mom's cabinet, in the local drug store, or in the sermons I hear at the church we've randomly attended since I was a little girl. The makeup I need the most I can't find.

And so, I've decided to write. Ever since I was little, when the teacher would give homework where we had to write about our vacations, or birthdays, or holidays, I felt I understood more after writing about something. I felt relieved. Things made more sense to me after I had to make sense out of them to others. God knows I need to make some sense out of my life now, so I'm writing. I've felt the need and urge to do other things as well, and my friends are getting more and more nervous about the cuts they've noticed on my arms. I'm just glad they can't see the rest of me, but I'm getting better and better at hiding. At hiding all kinds of things.

In the images that float before me, one of the most inviting ones is darkness. It's not the scary kind of darkness you felt when you were small and in your bedroom at night. This darkness is like a blanket that you can wrap around yourself to be warm and safe, to be free! It's kind of like dreaming, when for a little while you can be in another world and another reality, even though it's an illusion. Sometimes, this image is real appealing, and I feel a calmness that I can't find in the light. Sometimes, I want to become part of it, become formless and colorless, drift away like silver smoke in a breeze.

Different writers have meant a lot to me at different times growing up, from Judy Blume to Dr. Spock, and lately it's been Edgar Allen Poe. That must symbolize something, but I can't imagine that it's good. There's this particular one called "A Dream Within A Dream" and it seems real appropriate to me these days. It goes like this:

I stand amid the roar
of a surf-tormented shore,
And I hold within my hand
Grains of the golden sand...
How few! Yet how they creep
Through my fingers to the deep,
While I weep...while I weep!
Oh, God! Can I not grasp
Them with a tighter crasp?
Oh, God! Can I not save
***One** from the pitiless wave?*
*Is **all** that we see or seem*
But a dream within a dream?

Oh, yeah. Edgar wrote that one <u>just</u> for me. Now, if I could just find the answer.

CHAPTER 1

It was that changing of the seasons time at school again, the time when you've been back long enough that it's not as brutal a shock when the alarm goes off at 6:00 a.m. but it's still far from a welcome sound. November is the month when you mentally surrender to the inevitability of seven more months, mourn the loss of sunlight and warmth, try to make room for the onslaught of the holidays again, and watch the leaves turn dull brown, fall off the trees, and stick to the bottom of your shoes as you wait half-asleep for the bus in the dark cold rain of a fall morning.

The slow exodus of kids trudging to their respective bus stops every morning resembled a somber parade without any floats: heads down, backpacks slouching off the shoulders, grim resignation to the day's fate. The flashing lights of the big yellow beast as it groaned to a stop seemed garishly out of place with the overall gray decor of most of our school mornings in the northeast.

"I hate Mondays," Alisa said as we huddled under the street light.

"So do I. They suck, big time!" I concurred, as if we were having some kind of original thought that needed to be aired and shared. As Juniors, we'd been doing this for awhile.

"Are you ready for the math test today?" she asked, knowing my aversion to arithmetic.

"Yeah, sure!" I responded with more than a bit of sarcasm. "The next math test I'm ready for will be my first." Although Alisa and I had known each other since we were little and had shared the same corner for over a decade, our weekday morning reflections tended to be of few syllables and fewer original thoughts.

We climbed on and shuffled to our seats, about one-third the way down the aisle on the left, reserved for us by the inexplicable tendency of people to sit in the same seats after one day of random choice in early fall. We sat wearily and stared out the window at the same stores and the same houses we'd passed hundreds of times before. Conversation was not needed nor expected. As the belly of the beast slowly filled, stop by stop, the mood and level of alertness generally improved and the silence was gradually replaced by scattered chatter. Alisa and I talked with increasingly longer sentences about the day ahead, including the math test I wasn't really ready for that Alisa would probably ace, as she usually did. About twenty minutes later, the beast belched us out at the high school along with hundreds of others, and another school day began.

Marshall High School, a decent size school of about 1,200 students, had the reputation of being a "model school" because of the high scores its students tended to nail down on the standardized tests that can give a school fame or shame. Frankly, I thought it had more to do with the advantages that Marshall High kids were born with than with the academic acumen of the faculty, but my opinion was not solicited by the School Board nor the Administration for their carefully crafted, chest-thumping press releases.

The composition of the school had changed in the past ten years, and there were certainly more colors than white in the hallways these days. As we made our way to our lockers, I passed groups of kids who tend to cluster by race. The black kids hung with the black kids, the yellow kids with the yellow kids, the brown kids with the brown kids, the whites with the whites, and so on. We had a "People are a Rainbow" theme for a week at our school last year, which I guess would hold true if the colors all had their own separate arch over the sky. While I don't understand it, I've realized that I generally do the same. Lord knows we've talked about community, especially since we've had an increasing amount of conflict that was clearly color-based, gender-based, and status-based. Nobody, however, really seems to know what to do about it, and if "multicultural" means you do your thing and I'll do mine, then we're a real with-it school. Not that I don't associate with others. I have some friends who are different than me. However, there's some kind of distance that leaves a certain degree of awkwardness that we never quite overcome. It's strained, even when we don't want it to be. Makes me uncomfortable and I don't know what to do about it.

Homeroom? Well, now, that's an interesting concept. Someone will have to explain to me sometime what the hell home has to do with the room as we all sit there. Actually, someone could explain home to me as a concept in general. And then, understanding that, I could try to make the abstract leap to my connection with the "brothers and sisters" in homeroom. What does that make the teacher? Mom?

The second bell rang and I trudged to French. The hallways were like a crowded mall in the holiday season without the fun. Tara and I walked together, headed for the same class.

"How was your weekend?" Tara asked, making some hallway small talk. Tara and I had been in the same French class since middle school, and we had that kind of relationship that comes from coerced group membership. You know, where you like each other enough, but also know you wouldn't be close outside of that shared experience. Where you'd be OK if you ended up stranded together on a desert island but you wouldn't pick each other if you had a choice.

"Action packed, Tara. How was yours?"

"A two-day adventure, as always."

"So, you didn't do a damn thing either, huh?"

"Ah, nope!" she said with a smile.

As we were walking and talking, Jarvis passed with his troops, and we got our Monday morning greeting. "Hey, there, hos! How ya doing? Got any for me?" This was usually combined with the breast brushes, butt grabbing, snickering, etc., that completed the tribal ritual. Tara and I used to try to give him snotty, snappy replies but we found that it didn't have the desired affect, no matter how witty we were, so we gave up and just tried to get by as quickly as we could. Just for effect, however, Tara looked back at the boys with a sardonic glance and said something in a language that sounded like Spanish. I had no idea what she said, but I could tell it wasn't nice. The boys definitely looked confused by her comment, as there wasn't a linguist in the bunch, and Jarvis tried to recover with a loud, goofy laugh of contempt, pointing at us, but we snickered, knowing he'd been had and didn't even know it. Cerebral, he wasn't.

"<u>What</u> did you say to them?" I asked her.

She smiled slyly. "Oh, that? That was Spanish for 'Eat shit and die.' I like to look up dirty words in the language dictionaries in the library. You <u>never</u> know when they might come in handy."

"Oh, <u>nice</u>!" I commented. "I'm sure that's just what the School Board had in mind with our liberal education."

"Hey, did it come in handy, or what?"

"You couldn't have picked a more, how shall I say, perfect moment, girl!"

We got to French and took our seats. French was OK, and I'm pretty good at it. Ms. Slavik is real enthusiastic, and spoke French in an excited way that gave you the impression she invented it, even though she didn't come close to fitting the profile of a Parisian babe. She tried to generate enthusiasm for the subject, which a few students responded to, but most kids saw it as irrelevant. You know, the "What's the chance I'll ever be in France?" reasoning. She'd been teaching French for about a kazillion years and I wondered how she could drag herself in day after day to face the disinterest. True, I wasn't the only one in class who accepted the logic that it could possibly be helpful some day, but we "connoisseurs" were few.

I moved on to Math class, taught by Mr. Barbanis. He's a curious man, middle-aged, smaller than most of the boys and half of the girls. His round wire glasses sat nervously perched on his skinny nose, and the skimpy gray hair he did have left fell off the bald spot he futily tried to cover with it. He talked in random bursts as he furiously wrote math formulas on the blackboard, with some of us trying to keep up and the other half staring out the window, talking and fooling around, or sleeping. I was finding math harder and harder, and I ended up watching his mouth move when he was talking to us, trying to keep the abstract logic straight in my head. After awhile, it was like some hypnotic drone that lulled me like a mind-numbing mantra.

He passed out the math quiz I was so looking forward to, and I tried to make sense out of the problems staring up at me, whispering to me in a menacing way, "Go ahead! Figure us out. We dare you!" I doodled some numbers, added, subtracted, divided, and so on until it looked like I gave a shit and handed it in when Mr. Barbanis called time. He banged the handed-in papers until they were a nice symmetrical pile on his desk and proceeded to go over each problem, point-by-point, as he always did after a quiz. I proceed to float away, as I usually did.

After some time, from far away, I heard something that seemed to include my name in it. Again I heard it, and this time the voice was louder, more direct. "Molly! How did you arrive at your answer on number five?"

Panicked, I realized it was me he was talking to. I snapped to some kind of attention and fumbled with my papers, for no particular purpose. I was delaying the inevitable because I didn't have a clue, but what else was there to do?

"C'mon, Molly, we haven't got all day!" he said with increasing irritation. "Some time before the class is over!"

I stalled, dropped my notebook on the floor, croaked out a pitiful "Sorry!" and he looked more and more ticked.

"Forget it, Molly. Kevin, how did you do it? Oh, Molly, by the way, if you were wondering, you did it wrong."

No shit, Sherlock! I kinda figured that. Kevin gave the answer and I was off the hook. Math was symbolic of a lot of my classes these days. I couldn't stay focused, didn't give a damn, or actually thought I understood something only to bomb the tests.

A prime example was Social Studies, my next class. I used to get off on all that history stuff and thought it was kind of interesting. Now, I can't relate to the present let alone something that happened hundreds of years ago. Actually, it mostly seemed to confirm that humans have proven their stupidity over and over through time. If we're supposed to learn from our mistakes, we're one really slow species. History seemed so abstract, so distant, that it was almost surreal. Mrs. Phillips, who teaches social studies, tried to make it interesting by acting like past events were current, like talking in the present tense about ancient history, and using "we" instead of "they" when talking about the players involved. Nice try, but it didn't help much. Actually, it seemed kinda loopey and most of us thought she was weird. She wasn't that old, either, compared to the rest of the faculty, but it seems you age quick when you're teaching teenagers. She sometimes tried to act like she was a kid herself, but most of us just patronized her without her realizing it. She thinks she's cool, and we mostly let her go on with that myth.

Art? Art had possibilities. While I hated the mundane, childish "color and paste" type of projects we often got, there were some times when we got a chance to create, to express, to do something that met our own standard of meaning rather than some cut-and-dried total of right vs. wrong. Mr. Chilson seemed like an aging hippy who really got into the art. "When you use you heart, you make art!"

was his favorite saying. He was into long hair at a time when long hair on a guy really dated you. He exposed us to a lot of different art forms, and we had the chance to do clay works one week. I found myself lost in it. As I molded it with my hands and rolled it between my fingers, I felt that I was flowing into it, that my feelings were in the form. I wasn't even sure what it was, but it was me. Me! Not what I was told to be, what others expected me to be, but me. I didn't even know what the hell that was, but for a brief moment I felt it. Like art, it seemed to have possibilities.

The lunch bell rang, and the various tribes converged for the midday feeding: the Preps, the meticulously groomed kids in the primo button-downs and best-money-can-buy blouses; the Jocks, faster than a speeding bullet, strong enough to stop a train, and conceited enough to tell you so; the Skaters and the Goths, who desperately wanted to be noticed by proclaiming they didn't want to be noticed; the Stoners, burn-outs who slept <u>alot</u> and loudly in class; the Brains, who smiled condescendingly and confidently when we got the "wait-until-you-get-to-college" speeches; and the Unaligned, the huddled masses who either didn't claim allegiance to any one group or hadn't been fortunate enough to pass the various admissions tests.

Like most school-day markers, there were rules, procedures, and protocol to be followed; rules that were learned and internalized by day-to-day experiences that begin in elementary school on the playground, on the bus, in the locker room, and in gym; rules that dramatically elevated in importance in middle-school; and rules that were solidly internalized by high school through the ebb-and-flow of social reinforcement and punishment. Me, I felt like a group of one. (The Mollies?)

Not that I didn't apply for admission. However, it seemed like all I was able to do was accumulate an impressive pile of informal rejection slips. Some of the societies I applied to required you to submit to an initiation process where you walked, talked, dressed, and dined the same. Others called for capacities I either didn't possess or didn't give a shit about. Those that remained were kind of a losers' lot. (What's the old joke about not wanting to belong to any group that would be low enough to accept me as a member?) So I ended up kind of a floater - hanging wherever there was space to hang, sitting where there was a seat to sit in. Not that I was alone. There were others of the same ilk, and we often ended up together, but it usually seemed that we were the silt at the bottom of the pond. We tended to take some sort of perverse pride in our rejection, and we were proud of our pain. Take my lunch group, for example: Rebecca, Suzanne, Jennifer, Jasmine, and me, "the Lost Lunch Quintet." I'm not quite sure how we ended up as a lunch bunch, but we had been for some time.

"How's your day going?" Jasmine asked nobody in particular. She's kind of perky at times when the last thing in the world you want is perky. Tall, slender, and with eyes that absolutely sparkled with enthusiasm and interest, she was one of my few black friends and has been since we were little girls. We were friends at a time when skin color was no more than an interesting and curious difference to us, and we used to talk about it like we were comparing hair styles, or shoes, or backpacks. Back then, you could innocently ask questions about "How come?" and "Why?" without the political overtones they would take on in only a few more years.

While we both suffered through the realization that our differences were a much bigger social deal than we initially assumed, we'd managed to keep the core of our companionship intact. We were even able to actually talk about the "problem" a few times, especially one time in middle school when there were subtle (and sometimes not so subtle) pressures on both of us to stick with "our own kind." While I don't believe we were as tight as we once were, we still had an understanding that had endured. Also, her own personality was just so positive I think she just overwhelmed all the negatives staring us in the face. She still hung out with us alot, like at lunch, and we also knew a bunch of her black friends who I don't believe we would have if it wasn't for her. She was a bridge for me, and I believe I was for her, too. While I don't think the relationship was what it might have been if we were both of the same race, it was much more than our world seemed to want it to be. There was an unspoken symbolism for both of us that we knew was important, although we never mutually acknowledged it. Today, however, I couldn't take the positive vibes, no matter who they were coming from.

"Shitty. How's yours?" Rebecca answered sarcastically. Rebecca didn't do perky. As much as Jasmine was cheerful, Rebecca was cynical. Short dark hair, about six foot, she fit the mold of the proverbial stocky girl who takes-no-shit, but I think I would, too, if I had to put up with the lip she'd been taking over the years about her size. I'd seen her take some vicious taunts from both guys and girls, and sometimes teachers, too. I recall one situation in particular when we were outside after school in 7th grade and a bunch of the guys were playing touch football in the field beside the school. One of the real "popular" boys called over to Rebecca in a real loud voice, and asked her to be their middle linebacker. While we had no idea what that was, we all knew what it must symbolize when all the boys cracked up. She did her best to blow it off and act like she didn't give a damn, but I knew she died a thousand deaths. Rebecca's been swallowing this kinda stuff most of her life, so it wasn't hard to understand why she was, how shall I say, generally skeptical.

"Not bad. I think I did good on that Math test. How about you guys?" Perky wasn't easily discouraged by reality. We all gave Jasmine a you've-got-to-be-kidding look. She dropped it.

"Anybody got any weekend plans yet?" asked Jennifer, always looking forward. She was a "coordinator," a girl who needed to know what was on the calendar. She was as driven with the weekend plans as she was with her school work, and that was considerable. She was slight, with reddish blonde hair and blue eyes, and her little-girl face and physique had led many, both student and faculty, to underestimate her drive and determination. However, that usually only happened once, because underneath Jennifer was a dynamo who could and often did outdistance many of those around her. She wasn't a star, but she would wear you down with her persistence.

"Let me get through Monday, will ya?" barked Rebecca.

We munched on the same-old/same-old food and topics, and conversation lagged.

"I heard there's a party at Jack Ruthman's house," noted Suzanne. "His parents are going away for the weekend, and you <u>know</u> what <u>that</u> means. P-A-R-T-Y!" Her long, curly brown hair bounced as she talked a little louder than she needed to, and her glasses slipped a bit down her nose, like they always did when she got excited. She shuffled her short legs in eager anticipation and bounced on the bench, which looked kind of funny coming from a girl who looked more mature than she acted, with her impeccable outfits and pretty, preppy, face. If there was a social gathering to be found, Suzanne was the one to find it. She usually managed to sniff out some collection of kids doing something devoted to the relentless pursuit of a good time, and usually managed to get herself included in it. Personally, I worried that this party-proclivity she demonstrated was related to her tendency to drink whenever and wherever she could, despite her reputation to lose it easily and early. There were already a number of stories that began with "Did you hear about Suzanne...?" and were completed with details of barfing in various bushes, falling down in embarrassing places, and being deposited on her parents' porch with a hasty ringing of a doorbell followed by a pair or two of sneakers beating a hasty retreat. She'd then disappear from public view for some time due to subsequent groundings, etc. However, after awhile, it seemed her parents kind of gave up. She made it to most group events no matter what her previous week's transgressions had been.

"Are they ever home?" wondered Jasmine. Celebrations at Jack's house weren't exactly a novel or secret event. I'm expecting to see a neon-sign flashing "Jack's Secret Party Place" on his parents' porch one of these days.

"Will you be going?" Jennifer asked me. "I'm looking for a ride." She knew I just got my license and occasionally got the car.

"Damn right I'm going," I answered dryly. "I never miss a good party. That's me, party girl."

"Well, then, can you give me a ride?" Jennifer was nothing if not persistent.

"Yeah, sure, fine, <u>whatever</u>!" I could tell by the looks of my lunch mates that my crabbiness was a bit off-putting, but they should have been getting more used to it by then.

"What the hell's bothering you?" asked Rebecca.

"None of your goddamn business!" I snapped loudly, and the tension level went up a notch or two. It wasn't standard practice to challenge Rebecca, but I couldn't have cared less. One gets courageous when one doesn't give a damn.

"Hey, look sister, I'd be happy to kick your ass from here to tomorrow!"

"Fine, go ahead, have a <u>grand</u> old time!"

Rebecca tried to stare me down, but I suppose you had to stare back to make it go anywhere and, as I mentioned, I didn't give a damn, so after a few moments of stalemate the air seeped out of the show-down. Lunch returned to its pointless blah-blah-blah. The bell rang and the adventure began again.

When I got to my next class at the chemistry lab, Mr. Yenchak, the teacher, told me I was wanted in the guidance office. I hadn't exactly been a regular down in the counseling wing so this certainly tweaked my curiosity. When I got there and told the secretary that I was reporting as requested, she told me that Mr. Quinn, my guidance counselor, wanted to talk to me. After a brief wait, he called me into his office.

I knew Mr. Quinn through a couple of conversations about class schedules, class choices, and other academic minutia. His office had a bunch of rah-rah posters taped about extolling the virtues of hard work and deep study and predicting a good life for those who do both. (So that's my problem!) Mr. Quinn seemed like a nice enough man, about forty or so (but I have to admit I have a hard time guessing ages in those over thirty or so). One of the problems I've had with guidance types is that sometimes they get overly familiar way too quick. It's sort of like they'd like you to trust them and tell them everything when you hardly know them. Mr. Quinn fit the mold, and after a few warm-up questions about the weather, the holidays coming up, etc., we got into it.

"So, Molly, I've gotten some comments from a few of your teachers and friends that they're worried about you. They feel you haven't been yourself lately." There was a news flash. I hadn't felt like myself my whole damn life! "Want to talk about it?" he asked hopefully.

"Not particularly," I responded flatly.

He probed. "Sometimes, Molly, it can help to share some of this. Talking about the problem can help you deal with it."

"Really?" I wasn't going to give him anything.

"Yes, really." The silence got louder. He cleared his throat. "How are things at home? Any problems there?"

"No." Simple, to the point, untrue.

"How are your classes going? Some of your teachers said you seem distracted and that your grades are slipping."

"Really?"

"Yes, really." (Didn't we already do this scene?) By now, I was becoming increasingly aware of an annoying squeak from his old swivel leather chair in which he s-l-o-w-l-y rocked, back and forth, back and forth. The longer he talked, the louder the squeak to the point where it had to be up there with Poe's telltale heart. (Squeak-Squeak, Squeak-Squeak, Squeak-Squeak).

"Well, Molly, you need to remember that sometimes problems that seem so important right now won't seem so big when you get older. I kind of see you by yourself most of the time, and your teachers also notice you're alone a lot. You know, it might help if you get involved in some of the activities or clubs here at school. You might make some more friends and, actually, most of the students who are involved felt a bit more connected. You might even have some fun, and life may look a little better to you. What kinds of interests do you have?"

"What do you mean?" I wasn't biting!

"What do you like to do?"

"Sleep." No lie there.

"Other than sleep," he continued.

"Nothing."

"Nothing?" (He didn't believe me?)

"Yeah, nothing."

Mr. Quinn seemed to be squirming a bit by now. "Are there any other problems going on, like with your friends, a boyfriend, or something?"

"No."

"Well, Molly, I can't help you if you don't let me know what's bothering you."

"Oh, well." I really don't like to be snotty to others, especially those who I know are only trying to be nice, but come on! What did it take for this guy to get the message!

Again, the throat clearing. "All right, Molly, I can tell you really aren't up to talking about this." Finally! "However, we're all still worried about you, and I want you to know that you can talk to me at any time if you want." Not likely. "Also, I'd like to be able to talk to your parents about this a little bit."

I heard that! "Like hell! I don't want you talking to them! I'm fine, there's nothing to talk about!"

"Molly, you don't need to yell at me, I'm only trying to help. And you certainly don't need to curse at me!"

"Then let me get out of here and go back to class!" This was definitely going in a direction I did not want to travel. "I never asked to talk to you anyway!"

"OK, Molly, OK. I didn't want to make you angry. However, you need to know that we're obligated to tell somebody if we believe you're in bad shape."

"What do you mean, 'bad shape'? You can't tell anybody anything I tell you, can you? Isn't this supposed to be confidential?" I was moving from concern to panic.

"Actually, Molly, if we believe you might hurt yourself, we have to tell. We can't take that chance."

"Well, I'm not going to do anything! I never even thought about it!" Another lie.

"OK, Molly, please calm down. I'm not going to do anything right now. However, I'm going to give you the name of a psychologist I know who's pretty good with teens. You might talk to your parents about seeing him, or if it's easier I could talk to them for you. I still think you need to talk to someone, and it might be easier with somebody outside the situation whose trained to help with issues that are hard to talk to friends and family about."

"Fine, give me his name." I would have agreed to a public flogging to get out of his office. The posters were closing in on me. He gave me the shrink's office card, I stuffed it in my pocket, and fled.

Back in class for the afternoon, I found it even more difficult than usual to concentrate. The discussion with Mr. Harris had me rocked. I felt like I'd been "outed," but I suppose I was naive to think nobody else was going to notice. Funny how the only one you fool sometimes is yourself. But, for God's sake, I didn't want anybody talking to my parents! The last thing in the world I wanted was to have Mom and Dad going at it over this. When they can rip each other's lungs out over the time of day, I didn't want to be the center of their attention in a "discussion" that would certainly lead to another lovely knock-em-down. We kids had already been the subjects of most of their marital tugs of war and I sure didn't want to be the excuse for another one.

I also couldn't help but wonder which one of my "friends" ratted on me. Who had betrayed my confidence? Who had the goddamn nerve to go behind my back and put me in this position? Here I was, going out of my way to tell nobody anything, and someone decided to play God and blab to Guidance about my life! I was furious. I was nervous. I felt cheated.

After the trip home from school, I fell off the bus and crawled home. I'm alone for a few hours every day before anybody gets home, until Mom gets back from school, as the elementary school starts and finishes after the high school. I shuffled into my bedroom and collapsed on the bed. I keep my room dark, which isn't hard to do for most of the months where we live, and today was no exception. I also keep it quiet when possible, unless I'm trying to drown out the noise from the rest of the house, like when my Mom is home. I laid there and stared at the ceiling, the same ceiling I've stared at for more hours than I can count. Been here, done this.

The pain I was feeling was almost like some sort of perverted friend. I'd been feeling it long enough and strong enough that I knew it as well as I know myself, probably better. The hurt seeped its way into my bones, my muscles, and my back. My arms and legs started to shake, and I couldn't control my breathing. It always scared the hell out of me when I start to hyperventilate, giving me a feeling like my lungs were on a ventilator gone berserk. Faster, faster, and faster my lungs filled and deflated, and I was loosing control. I was panting like a freaking dog! The panting turned to panic and it flowed into every single inch of me, making it hard to see clearly. My hands and feet started to tingle with that prickly, electric feeling, and I was losing it, <u>big</u> time. I got up and paced around the bedroom, faster and faster. Desperate, I reached out and punched the top of my dresser, <u>hard</u>, and I didn't even feel it. I punched it again, and again, and again, and my knuckles started to bleed. The blood caught my attention, distracted me for an instant, but that's all. The panic grew, and I felt like I'd explode!

I knelt beside my bed and pulled out a wadded-up tissue from underneath. Frantically, I unwrapped it and took out the razor I kept there, shaking harder, breathing faster. Trembling, I gripped the razor in the middle between the two sharp edges, raised it, and slowly stroked it across my right arm, just below the elbow. As I did, the blood seeped up and flowed in rivulets following the path of the razor's edge as it opened my arm. The blood was dark red, almost maroon, as it rolled off the top of my arm, defying gravity while it curled to the opposite side before dripping onto the tissues underneath. Again and again, I pulled the blade across my arm until I couldn't distinguish one cut from the other.

As I watched my blood flow, my breathing slowed, and my heart stopped pounding out of my chest. My panic faded as the cuts started to throb, and my focus shifted from my shitty life to the curious wounds. It was as if all the hurt came together and congealed in my arm. It was lots better this way. My own blood was a sedative. It was <u>lots</u> better this way. I got zoned staring at the blood, hypnotized, mesmerized, carried away. The pulsing in my arm beat to a slow rhythm that was soothing, reassuring. The rest of world faded away and all that was left, all that I could see, all that I could feel was my arm, the blood, and the pain. No Mom and Dad; no Mr. Harris; no school; no friends; and no enemies. It was <u>lots</u> better this way. <u>Lots</u> better......lots better.........better.........

I came to as if slapped in the face when I heard Mom's car pulling in the driveway. I had no idea how long I was out, no idea what time of day it was, but it was dark now. Panicked again, I grabbed the bloody razor and stuffed it in the dark-red tissues, still wet and sticky. I tossed it under my bed again, and realized that my blood leaked onto the rug. No time now! Think quick! The car door slammed. Grab a towel from the bathroom! Hurry up! Throw it on top of the blood! Did I get it all??? Run into the bathroom and flush the toilet, it'll buy some time! Rinse my arm and hands off under the cold water. It stings! Find an old towel in the closet and wrap it around my arm, I can deal with the blood stains later. Damn, the arm won't stop bleeding! Press harder, harder! What about my jeans? Shit! Blood stains on them, too! Wipe them off, wet the towel with <u>cold</u> water, that works best! OK, OK, stay calm. Got to change the blouse, I'm wearing short sleeves! Careful, don't get blood on the blouse. Put on a big sweatshirt, that'll work good! Blood won't seep through either if I start bleeding again. All right, that's good. How do I look? Terrible! She'll know I'm up to something! What can I do? I have to go downstairs, or she'll come up, and I haven't cleaned the rug yet! OK, I can do this. STAY CALM, DAMMIT!

"Hi, Mom." So far, so good. She was distracted, looking at the mail, checking the fridge for dinner possibilities.

"Hi, Molly, how was your day?"

"Fine, Mom." Yeah, right!!

"Anything new at school today?"

"No, Mom." Yeah, right!! "Look, Mom, I'm kinda tired and not real hungry, so I'm gonna take a nap. I'll have something to eat when I get up, OK?"

"C'mon, Molly, you hardly eat anything anymore. Have something to eat first."

"Mom, I'm not hungry. I'll eat something when I get up, I promise." Promises, promises.

"OK, Molly, but I'll wake you up in an hour or so. You won't be able to sleep tonight if you sleep too long now." If she only knew.

"OK, Mom." I went back to my room, locked it, and took the sweatshirt off to check on my cuts. They were an angry-looking series of jagged, purple-red streaks, but the bleeding had pretty much stopped, just a bit caked along the edges. Again, I wiped them off with a cold washcloth, and now they were really starting to hurt and throb. It was comforting to know that for awhile my mind could shut down, go off-line, and let the throbbing take over. I put the sweatshirt back on carefully, so as not to start the cuts bleeding again, and I laid on my bed, staring at that same old ceiling again. My breathing kind of got into a rhythm with the throbbing, and it calmed me. I stared at the ceiling, numb, blank, floating. The image of darkness came to me again, like a fog rolling over a hill when the weather changes. I was thinking nothing, feeling nothing. *It's OK. It's OK. It'll be OK.*

CHAPTER 2

Home is one of those "loaded" words that you learn to understand on a multitude of levels with a million different meanings, most of which depend on variables over which you have little control. For example, for me (and for most of my friends), home depended on whose weekend it was. I suppose we were like the "typical American family" - it was with Dad every other weekend and Mom all the other times, except for the alternating holidays and several weeks over the summer.

I was eight when they divorced and my brother, Joshua, was ten. I remember when they sat us down for "the talk." It's interesting, but when I've discussed this with my friends whose parents are divorced, they shared basically the same scenario. Their parents, too, wanted to believe that they were letting them in on something that they didn't already know. Despite the fights (loud and not so loud), the silences, the "let's make up and be like we used to be" weekends that rarely made it through the whole two days, the unexpected not-Christmas time gifts that they gave us out of guilt, and the <u>tension</u>, Mom and Dad told us that Dad would be moving out as I imagine a doctor would tell somebody they had cancer. And, even though I knew it was coming, I did feel I was told I had a terminal illness. After all, our family was dying, wasn't it?

I'm not sure which emotion I felt the most at that time, but I can tell you I had a bunch of them, none good. Mostly, I was heartbroken. I still am. I always will be. I lost something I can never replace and, in some ways, something I never really had. As long as I can remember, it was strained (at least) between Mom and Dad. However, as a kid, you always have hope. Maybe this time, things will get better. Maybe this time, the counseling will help. Maybe this time, they'll work it out. Or, maybe not.

In some ways, I felt a strange combination of relief and guilt. I was relieved because at last there would be some kind of closure to this cold war. I remember sitting in a Social Studies class when we were discussing some stupid war or another where people kept fighting and killing each other for years and years, and still do. I couldn't help but think of "home sweet home" where the battle lines were drawn over the kitchen table, or the checkbook, or the holidays or, worse yet, me and Joshua; where the skirmishes were waged with the family weapons of choice, which included any emotional brick that could be thrown. And, as in every war, innocent bystanders were hit by friendly fire. Josh and I both had the scars to show for it. So, yes, I was relieved. And I hated myself because of that.

I felt guilty because….well, I'm not really sure why but I did (and do!). Certainly, some of the arguments before the divorce and most of them afterwards were about me and my brother. What else was there to fight about? I felt guilty because the stuff we needed was something else to argue about. I felt guilty because no matter which parent I was with, the other was hurt because I wasn't there. I felt guilty because, many times, I didn't want to be there. And now, I felt guilty because, late at night, when I thought about how I wanted my life to be, I prayed it would be anything as long as it wasn't like theirs.

But, time rolls on. (Thank God!) All these years later, life seemed to approximate some kind of normal, which I was beginning to appreciate was a real relative state of being. My parents were well into their mid-life crises, with Dad at 43 and Mom not far behind at 42. The aging of Steven Mitchell and Margaret Wooding. (Mom went back to using her maiden name.) So, there I was, last name Mitchell, with my mom, last name Wooding. It sort of made it hard to feel "family" when you had different last names floating around in the house.

My mom is an 3rd grade elementary school teacher. You know what they say about grade school teachers. After awhile, they treat <u>everyone</u> like gradeschoolers. The same was true for my Mom. She had this way of calling everyone "sweetheart" that was both infuriating and enduring at the same time. I guess this could have a different impact on the receiver depending on one's age, gender, or status, but Mom seemed to pull it off without any public relation problems.

She never remarried. While I was certainly not party to the particulars of the divorce, I sensed that it was more Dad's idea than Mom's. She had a sadness about her that never seemed to leave her altogether, though sometimes I saw it lighten a bit when she was engrossed in a fun project with her students or when my brother and I were doing something fun with her, like watching a silly movie that we might rent or shopping for souvenirs at the beach on a vacation. At those times, she had a lift in her laugh, or did or said something "goofy," which was <u>definitely</u> not like her. It didn't last long enough, though, before the clouds rolled in again. She tried dating a few times but it seemed like it was more work than fun. Also, most of the guys who were available were divorced themselves (which was why they were available!) and Mom said she'd already had enough of that scene that she didn't want to inherit somebody else's problem. So, she was lonely. By choice? By fate? By bad luck? I don't know! In many ways, it kind of seemed like divorce was the ultimate death of optimism.

My friends really like Mom. For her age, she was still pretty, with long dark hair showing only a hint of gray (which she promised she'd have dyed as soon as it was noticeable!) and a decent shape (for her age). Physically, she looked pretty young, although sometimes when it was late and I was going to bed or coming in on a weekend, she looked anything but. It was hard to tell if it was fatigue or loneliness, or both. She liked having my friends around the house, which was rare compared to my friends' parents (who also liked me having my friends around my house). She seemed to enjoy the company.

It gets a bit heavy sometimes wondering about my relationship with my Mom. Am I a daughter, a sister, a confidant, or some strange hybrid of the three? I know she didn't have a lot of other friends to talk to, but I wandered back and forth from feeling special and older to uncomfortable and cornered. I respect the way she's been able to juggle both raising us and her job but it was hard to not felt like a burden sometimes. Not that Mom had done anything overt to make us feel that way. If anything, I think she felt more guilt than anything about what we hadn't been able to do over the years. It put me in an awkward position sometimes. I felt it was my job to make her felt better and sometimes, I wondered whose job it was to make me feel better. Kinda selfish, don't you think?

Mom also had a core of bitterness that those outside the family rarely saw, but we did. She had a hair-trigger where anything involving my Dad was concerned, and we've learned from experience to avoid giving the impression of aligning with the "dark side." Her anger and hurt lived close to the surface, and either she didn't realize how easily both bubbled out or had given up trying to contain them. There also wasn't anyone else in her life to express it to besides us. When you're a kid living in that situation, you learned when to "duck," when to get the hell out of the line of fire. We definitely pussyfooted around her at those times because she got a look in her eyes that let you know she could do some real damage, with a tongue that was barbed and baited. We'd felt its sting a number of times.

These dynamics changed dramatically every other weekend. Then, I morphed into a combination of daughter, stepdaughter, sister and stepsister. My brother and I stepped into an altogether different environment at Dad's.

Dad has always lived two different lives (at least!). When we were little, his job as a sales rep for a large retailer kept him on the road for days, sometimes weeks at a time. We got used to Mom being the one who went to our open houses at school, helped us (or made us) get our science projects done, or stayed up with us when we were sick at night. When Dad was home, the atmosphere changed. He was always a couple of steps behind us, trying to catch up. Oh, sure, he really tried, and even once volunteered to help coach Josh's basketball team when Josh was in sixth grade. Josh, however, said he had a hard time getting used to it, and seemed nervous about doing something wrong. After all, he didn't get many opportunities to impress Dad.

When Dad was able to make it to the practices, he and Josh would both leave the house excited and pumped, only to come home silent and serious. I was never sure what happened, but at the weekly games I watched it seemed that Josh had a hard time sharing Dad with all the other kids and Dad seemed determined to not show any favoritism to Josh. The combination didn't work real well. They both seemed relieved when the last game was over. The next season, they both avoided the topic of Dad coaching altogether, although Dad went to all the games he could.

Dad remarried two years after the divorce. I'm not really sure when he and Cindy got involved, and he hasn't exactly been forthcoming about the timeline, but there was that weekend some months after he left where we were "introduced." I guess I shouldn't have been surprised. Dad's a decent looking guy, tall with the nice-looking gray hair that some men get when they get older. He's managed to stay in shape working out at the hotels he lives half his life in. Dad's got an easy way around people, like some salesman have. I've always wondered if people go into sales and become real smooth talkers, or if they go into sales for that reason in the first place.

Cindy is a few years younger than Mom, kinda pretty, and certainly nice enough. Sometimes, I wish she wasn't so nice. I wouldn't have to wrestle with these mixed feelings about her, I could just hate her!

At the time, Dad seemed a bit uncomfortable trying to explain the particulars of what was to take place. He nervously explained that even though he and Mom both loved us, he felt it was time "to get on with my life," and I remember wondering where Josh and I figured in that equation. He explained that he had met someone, "made a new friend," and he wanted us to meet her.

Cindy came over for dinner that afternoon, and it helped explain the nagging suspicions Josh and I had been carrying around like a bug bite for some time. Often, parents are desperate enough or guilty enough to believe that which they want to believe, and Dad wanted to believe that we knew nothing about his new relationship, despite the feminine signs posted about his apartment. Sometimes, we kids play along, and Josh and I did our part to walk carefully, silently, and obediently around yet another elephant in the living room. At this point, we were experienced. Besides, we didn't want to hear it any more than he wanted to tell us, so youthful ignorance was just fine with us! However, we were now face-to-face with a reality we had no frame of reference to process, no code to help with the translations, and no program to explain how the show was to go. Actually, as a child, you tend to assume that your parents will help you deal with the anxieties and uncertainties you face as you confront the new and unknown, and there is the security of a net stretched below you that helps you sleep securely in the dark, trusting that it's OK because your parents are behind you, emotionally holding you, protecting you from the spooky things that terrify because you can't understand. In this situation, we were on our own. No net.

A couple of weekend visits later, Cindy stayed instead of going back to her place, and Dad must have guessed we were all chummy enough at this point that it wouldn't be a problem. Wrong! More wishful thinking. While we weren't stupid enough or naive enough to believe they weren't "getting it on," it was a bit easier to handle my father's premarital sex when it wasn't happening down the hall. I mean, really, it's disturbing enough when you first realize that your own parents sweat up the sheets, let alone trying to process it happening between your dad and somebody you don't even know. We all muddled through it, pretended it was all right, survived a tension and awkwardness that was in many ways unbearable. Actually, after awhile, it was sort of nice. Dad struggled to create a "we're a new family" atmosphere and we played along (again!). Our weekends were action-packed, and Dad made sure we had places to go and stuff to do. Josh and I also weren't above the practice of manipulating the situation, either, and Mom came to know that if she wasn't happy with us, or what we did, didn't do, or wanted to do, then perhaps Dad and Cindy would be. It was a perverted reversal of power and emotional control that we weren't supernatural enough to walk away from and certainly too young to control.

Inevitably, however, time takes the shine off of everything and all that's left are people; people with choices, opinions, and feelings; people with histories, pressures, and beliefs about how things are supposed to be; people with wounds and bruises, and worries about getting hurt again; people with hopes for the future and fears about what might shatter those hopes; and people we think we know and trust, and people we don't.

One of the factors that helps us cope with these personal ambiguities is a decent definition of what our respective roles are. For example, while I may not always agree with my Mom, she's still my Mom. You know, the person who gave birth to you and so on. Even my brother gets the benefit of biology! But what about a stepmother? A stepdaughter? How does one define these roles? Where are the models to give us a clue? I find it amazing that despite the fact that I know as many kids whose parents are divorced as those who aren't, we act like everybody comes from a big happy family. Well, hello! We don't! So, we stumble along wondering if we're friends or family, and end up as foes.

Cindy tried to be motherly but I let her know in no uncertain terms that I already had one. We fumbled along with the small talk over the dinners, tried to do "girl stuff" together, and had a variety of situations where we were on the opposite sides of a dispute that placed my Dad solidly in the middle of a no-win situation. Ultimately, it seemed that he weighed the reality of a few more years of occasional day-to-day life with me versus the rest of his life with Cindy. Guess who won?

Josh navigated his own course through these family mazes, and it hasn't been any easier for him. Initially, he was adequately comfortable with the living arrangements and coped with the coming and going of parents and problems, furniture and futures. However, his relationship with Mom became strained when he was about 13. He became less than cooperative with Mom's limits, and he was increasingly willing to battle with her. Eventually, it reached a point where he was physically bigger than Mom, looking a whole lot like Dad. I don't think that made the situation any better, and I had difficulty telling if he was acting like Dad did towards her because we watched Dad do it so many times or if Mom treated him as if he was a reincarnation of Dad, kind of a guilt by physical association. In many ways, I think Josh reminded her of Dad, and she was exacting revenge in abscentia. Shortly after, he started talking to me about wanting to spend more time with Dad and then, not long after that, he started talking (loudly at times) to Mom about the same theme. This was particularly true when they were in the heat of a disagreement, which was all too frequent. He learned that it was a potent weapon to threaten Mom with moving to Dad's, and she <u>always</u> took the bait!

The heartbreaker for Josh came the weekend shortly after his 14th birthday when we were at Dad's. It had been a particularly bad week between Josh and Mom after some negative notes were sent home from school, and Josh asked Dad if he could move in with him and Cindy. I think it took a great deal of courage on Josh's part to ask, because he was emotionally risking everything. The puzzled look on his face when Dad said that wasn't possible was quickly replaced by shock when Dad told him the reason. He and Cindy just found out she was pregnant, and there wouldn't be enough room in their house when the baby came.

This news blew me away but I think it devastated Josh. He had been identifying more and more with Dad the past couple of years but, in one short announcement, it was made abundantly clear that our stock was going to plummet! How many different ways can a parent be split? How the heck many roles were we expected to act out? What, exactly, were we supposed to do with this? There's Dad telling us with this big smile, like there's any particular reason this should be good news for us. It was almost as if he could just will it to be positive for us. And there we were, left feeling jealous, jilted, and conflicted.

The six months before the delivery were really strange. As Cindy got bigger and bigger, and Dad spent more and more time getting their new home ready for the baby, I felt more and more awkward. If I didn't felt like I was crashing somebody else's party before, I sure felt that way now. I was getting this naggingly bad taste in my mouth about the whole thing, and I kind of flinched when I realized I was chewing on resentment. I don't like feeling negative things about other people, and I particularly didn't care for having this sense about my father. But, try as I might, I couldn't shake it, and I sure couldn't find a way to bring it up with my friends (too weird) and I didn't dare mention it to my mother (<u>way</u> too weird!).

Dad and Cindy tried hard to involve us in the event, and Dad tried to assure us that he'd still be there for us, and nothing would really change. We had a hard time understanding how that could be. There was the expected speculations about whether it would be a boy or a girl, and they worked to excite us about an event that really had nothing to do with us. Actually, I take that back. I guess it had <u>everything</u> to do with us, but not in any way that I could look forward to.

It seemed really strange to me that the first baby shower I got to attend was that of my stepmother. As a young girl, I used to think about, dream about, and look forward to the time when I'd be old enough to be involved in these type of events. Looking back on it, it seems that you prepare yourself for what you might experience and feel when your time comes by watching what those older than you experience when they go through it. However, not in my wildest dreams did I think it would be like this! There I was with a bunch of women I didn't know (Cindy's side of the family) along with my Aunt Maureen (Dad's sister) and a few cousins I had sporadic, holiday-visit involvement with in the past. I watched as Cindy opened the gifts while all the ladies "oohed" and "ahhed" as each gift was eagerly unwrapped. She looked so happy and excited, and I tried to be happy for her but all I could feel was uncomfortable. I was relieved when it was over.

I didn't really care whether it was a boy or a girl. Frankly, by this point, I really didn't care, <u>period</u>. (Pretty crude, don't you think?) I don't think Josh felt the same way, though, and, wouldn't you know it? Dad and Cindy had a boy! Named him Michael (Dad's middle name). They made a lovely family.

I guess Michael was your typical baby. Cried <u>alot</u>, slept alot, spit up alot. Babies sure looked like a lot of work, and it was strange to see Dad changing a diaper, walking the floor in the middle of the night, and carrying Michael proudly in a backpack. He looked a little old for the job. Also, while I'd have a hard time telling you anything I can actually remember about my infancy, I don't recall any yellowing pictures in the family album of Molly or Josh riding the paternal camel. Too bad. I suspect his back would have been able to handle the stress better the first time around, but we'll never know. Cindy was <u>beaming</u>, and her need and attempts to be motherly with us sure waned. Their house became a nursery, and two visiting teenagers didn't match well with the decor. You know the old saying—- three's company, five is two plus three.

Michael's four now, and a cute kid. It feels a bit bizarre to be jealous of a preschooler. However, I'm not into Sesame Street anymore, and "Barnie" makes me want to barf! Dad and Cindy go gaga over all the milestones, and Kodak must be making a fortune on this kid! Our accomplishments couldn't compete with first steps, first words, first "potty poops." And so, I find myself again with that bad taste in my mouth, and the mouthwash ain't working. How does that old song go? "Be it ever so humble, there's no place as goddamn confusing as home."

CHAPTER 3

It was Friday night, which was supposed to symbolize some sort of weekly American adolescent "coming out" ritual. Usually, however, it meant crushing boredom and a desperate search for something to do to recapture some lost sense of freedom and opportunity. So, like any self-respecting teen, I tried when I could, so when the inevitable inquiry of "What did you do over the weekend?" rolled my way, I'd have something to say. Mom was in a generous mood and I had the car. I pulled out of the driveway and swung over to Jennifer's to pick her up. We were good to go, and Mom had been comforted and placated with a convenient fable about a sleepover. Jenn and I chatted about nothing in particular on the way over to Jack's party.

We pulled into Jack's neighborhood, a relatively new development with upscale homes, and it was hard to find a place to park by his house. There was a crowd already! We cruised around until we found a spot. The cold fall wind was blowing back our hair as we hustled over to his house, and we could hear the music blasting several houses away. (Nothing suspicious going on here!) We rang the doorbell, waited, but no one came as the sound of the chimes was swallowed up by the rap music blaring inside. We rang it again - still no response. Getting colder, we just opened the door and stepped into a foyer where the noise level went up dramatically. Walking down the hall we passed kids in the living room all clinging to red plastic cups, talking loudly and seemingly all at once. The smell of beer was strong as we walked towards the kitchen. The kids we knew called out as we passed, and Suzanne spotted us and yelled, "Hey, Jenn, Molly, over here! Over here! Grab a beer." She was in the family room off the kitchen with another group. As we got closer, I noticed the glassy-eyed look of someone who had a few. "G-r-e-a-t party," she pronounced, slurring the words, sounding like my Great Uncle Frank after his stroke as she waved her cup around precariously.

"Hang on, Suzanne, give us a chance to catch up, will ya?" asked Jennifer.

"C'mon, c'mon, <u>c'mon</u>!" she pleaded, "I don't want to be ripped all by myself!" However, the ridiculous grin on her face indicated that our absence hadn't been a social roadblock for her. Also, judging by the group mood and voice volume, she wasn't "ripped" all by herself.

We mooched our way through the crowd around the keg, procured a couple of cups, and filled them from a half-filled pitcher on the kitchen table. I chugged mine down in one big gulp. When I was fourteen, I discovered at a family Christmas party that I had the less-than-feminine ability to swallow multiple ounces of the amber fluid without stopping for air. I tapped this talent to close the distance between me and my inebriated peers, filling and then draining the cup several times in short order. Since my holiday introduction to booze, I've had several opportunities to partake as it's not exactly hard to find a party or to siphon off the parental stash. I've also discovered that I can drink as much as most of the guys and, in some cases, more. I'm not sure if this is because it takes me longer to get a buzz, or just longer to stop feeling anything. Whatever the case, I've recognized the medicinal potential and have employed it several times since. While it seems I inevitably ended up with nothing more than a bad headache, long episodes in the bathroom hugging the toilet, and some interesting alibis for my mother, I relished the escape, however brief. Drinking enables me to be something I'm not - confident, funny, and fearless. It also helps me do things I generally can't do, such as believe in myself. It may be a lie, but what the hell!

The three of us went and hogged the couch in the family room, drinking and chatting, laughing, getting more and more "relaxed." Various conversations popped up with kids who stopped by, some we knew, some we didn't. A beer here and a beer there, and eventually all the edges softened. I was damn near mellow, witty, "urbane" (<u>cool</u> word - heard it in a movie once - have no idea what it means but it seemed to fit). Suzanne wasn't looking so good and excused herself for another trip to the john. Her spot on the couch wasn't vacant too long before this boy showed up and asked, "This seat available?"

Here was a dilemma! This kid was cute, with light brown hair a bit on the long side, blue eyes, skinny. He seemed casual in a friendly kind of way. There also were no other seats available, and I had no idea where the hell Suzanne was. I pondered this problem briefly with my increasingly foggy reasoning skills before I answered with deep insight. "Actually, we're saving it for a friend." Simple, to the point, <u>true</u>!

I figured I was doing real well here, feeling real smug (which is also easier under the influence) when Jenn complicated the situation by saying, "I'm gonna go check on Suzanne. I'll be back in a minute." With that, she jumped up and left! Now here I was with <u>two</u> spots available.

I looked up at this guy and he was standing there with this smug smile on his face. "Still no room?"

"My friends should be back in a minute," I answered sheepishly. "You could just end up evicted."

"I'll take my chances, if that's OK with you. I've been standing <u>all</u> <u>night</u>! I don't know if you noticed but it's <u>packed</u> here! I just want to sit down for a minute. When your friends come back, I'll go away. I promise!"

I don't know how you're supposed to judge an "honest face," (which, when you think of it, is one of the stupidest concepts ever conceived), but alcohol seemed to make the world look more brotherly (or sisterly, if you will). I took him at his word. "Have a seat."

"Thanks alot." He plopped down on the couch, sitting at one end after I scooched over to the other. We sat there for awhile, each of us trying to act like the other wasn't there when in reality we were <u>acutely</u> aware. It's kind of like being in an elevator with only one other person, where you are intensely conscious of the fact that no one is talking and no one else is there. However, on an elevator you eventually get off at some floor. Me and this guy, we were just sitting there, feeling more and more awkward. The couch seemed to be getting smaller, down to about love-seat size by now.

He broke first. "So, uh, do you come here often?" He grinned at the lack of originality in his opening line.

"I can't exactly say I'm a regular," which was true enough. "You?"

"I'm a friend of a friend of a friend of a......well, you get the picture."

"I don't think you're alone. There's a whole lot of people here I don't know."

"Me, too."

Silence again. Awkward again.

Finally, "I'm Craig."

"Molly."

"Nice to meet you."

"Uh, huh."

"What happened to your friends? They were both here and then they were both gone."

"One's not feeling real good, and the other went to check." By the way, where the hell were they?

"Too much party?"

"Maybe. I'm not sure."

We continued to just sit there and I had that mute-like feeling where you desperately want to find something witty to say, or funny, or relevant, and end up hoping to think of something, <u>anything</u>, but no dice. It feels like your head fills up with words and thoughts, all jumbled together, and the more you try to disentangle them, the more snarled they become and eventually your head starts to hurt from the strain.

"So, where do you go to school?" Craig asked. Not exactly a show-stopper but I guess you gotta start somewhere.

"I go to Marshall. Where do you go?"

"Actually, I go the Central. I'm a Senior there but I've got friends from Marshall. Mitchell Lewis is a pretty good friend. Do you know him?"

Like he was talking to a social magnet. "I know of him. He's a Senior, though. I'm a Junior. Lower life form."

"Oh, that's OK. A lot of my friends are Juniors."

"Well, I don't have a lot of friends who are Seniors."

All right, somebody could help me with this stuff. Talk about confusing. How does one go about this boy-girl interaction business? Who leads? How do you follow? I've had some of the best education taxes can buy, but nowhere do I recall any discussion about how one is to handle this. And let's face it, what's one of the big topics we're all interested in developmentally at one time or another? That's right, "How to deal with the opposite sex when you're in the adolescent might-be-interested stage and can't think of a damn thing to say." But did I get that? No! Instead, I got foreign languages which were likely to stay foreign, and math that I haven't seen anybody anywhere use other than in math class, and earth science about cosmic events that were really, you know, cosmic, and so on and so on. Big, fat, hairy help they were then, when I needed a solid grounding in Relationships 101!

Craig cracked first. "So how do you like Marshall?"

Now I realized that this guy was trying to make conversation, so I wasn't going to stuff the real answer down his throat. "Fine. How's Central?"

"It's a school," he responded. "You know, school's school."

"Ya got that right."

Silence again. Then, "These parties are kinda dumb," he suggested.

"Why's that?"

"Oh, I don't know. It kinda feels like everyone's trying to act more ripped than the next person. There's a lot of 'posers' here."

"So, why are you here?" A bit brazen, perhaps, but he brought the subject up.

"I don't know! All right, I admit it's stupid to dis the party while I'm sitting here drinking, too, but what else is there to do?

"Not a whole lot, I guess." We were rolling now!

"I don't exactly know a lot of people here, either."

"Neither do I."

"Really? Well, at least it's your school. You go there with most of these kids, don't you? Aren't most of them from Marshall?"

"Yeah, but that doesn't mean I know a lot of them. We're kind of a big school. Besides, everybody sort of stays in their own groups."

"And what's your group?" he asked.

Now there was the million-dollar question! "I haven't got one," I answered honestly.

"Funny," he said with a look of true bonding, "Neither do I."

Now, I could have been all wrong here, as I wasn't exactly a veteran in this field, but I was beginning to think that this guy seemed interested in Molly Mitchell! Even more amazing, Molly didn't want to hurl! What the hell was wrong with this picture? Where the hell were Suzanne and Jennifer? What do I do now? Inquiring minds wanted to know.

Boys, dating, relationships and all that good stuff have been a source of bewilderment for me for as long as I can remember. As a little girl, I would see some of the teenagers in the neighborhood "pairing off," and they seemed so old to me, so big. In middle-school, kids would talk about "going out" with so-and-so, although it was mostly all talk and no action. Relationships that were established in the a.m. were extinguished in the p.m. (with the possible exception of a few "adventerous" girls who were hot-to-trot and running with older guys). Didn't impact me. Then we all made the transition to high school, and you kind of wondered, what now? How does this whole dating thing work? Do you just kind of wait around and it somehow comes to you, or are you supposed to file an application, look for a sponsor, advertise, or what? Is it expected, like taking phys-ed? Are you doing something wrong if it doesn't happen? Or is there something wrong with you? It didn't seem to be a problem for some kids, and they seemed to deal with a.) not having, b.) getting, and c.) losing relationships just fine. No big deal. Easy come, easy go. For many of us, though, it was a private club with secret rituals, hidden doors, and passwords we couldn't decipher. It's not that we weren't interested. We just couldn't crack the damn code!

In my two and a half years of high school, I had some interactions that made me wonder, made me curious, even made me wonder if somebody else was curious, but nothing ever developed. I sort of assumed that boys weren't interested in me unless it was the random uninvited grab-ass incidents that happen accidentally on-purpose. Hell, I'm not interested in me! Who could possibly see me as relationship material? Ugly is as ugly does. And yet, there I was. One-on-one. Me and a boy. Talking not because we had to but because we wanted to. Holy shit! Isn't alcohol a wonderful thing? As I was pondering these mysteries of life, Jenn showed up. "Where the hell have you been?" I whispered with impatience.

"Where the hell do you think? I got up to go to the bathroom and came across Suzanne in the process. She was busy barfing in the john. She's not looking real good so I stuck around with her for awhile. She's laying down in one of the bedrooms but she needs to go home, Molly." Jenn had a bit of mothering in her.

"How about you, Jenn? How are you feeling?"

"Not bad. I didn't drink that much."

Goddamn! I was boy-bonding here for the first time in my miserable life and we had to go? Figured. "I can give you guys a ride home," I volunteered. Might as well face the music. "Let's go."

Jenn sized up my newfound friend on the couch with me. "Who's your buddy?" she asked quietly while eyeing up Craig.

"I'm Craig," he volunteered. "How are ya?" This boy was paying attention.

"Freaking great, Craig, freaking great!" Jenn looked pissed.

"This is my friend, Jennifer."

"Nice to meet you, Jennifer." Polite bloke, this Craig.

"Yeah, great, Craig," she answered with mild irritation. Jenn's mood wasn't improving here.

Heavily, I said "C'mon, Jenn, let's go." The party was over.

Jenn did a quick visual scanning of my situation here and said, "Don't worry about it. Kevin Branch said he'd give us a ride." Possible reprieve? Dead girl walking?

"Are you sure? What kind of shape is he in?"

"He's fine. Kevin doesn't drink."

"Are you sure?" Survivor guilt?

"With the 'sure' thing again! Yes, I'm sure!"

"OK, OK, don't get pissed at me, Jenn. I never said I wouldn't give you a ride if you need it. What did I do?"

Jennifer softened a bit. "Nothing, Molly, nothing. It's not your fault. You and, uh…. What's your name again?" she asked, pointing to Craig.

"Craig," he answered, mildly amused.

"That's right. You and Craig keep on keeping on and I'll go home with Suzanne. Don't worry about it, we'll be fine. Just don't asked me 'Are you sure?' again, OK?"

I was no fool. "I am sure," I said with a grin. She left, and I felt guilty that I didn't even get up to go check on Suzanne before they left, but Mother Jennifer could take care of her, or at least that's how I rationalized it to myself.

"So," said Craig, "alone again."

"Yeah, us and dozens of party partners," I said with a gesture to the huddled masses in various stages of inebriation.

"Want to go for a walk? Get a little cold air to wake us up? A little nocturnal exercise?" he asked.

"OK, what the heck, I've about had enough stale beer and cigarette smoke to last a while." I figured this would either cure me or kill me.

"Where's your coat?" he inquired.

"In the front room upstairs in a heap with all the other coats".

He jumped up and asked, "Want me to get it for you?" Helpful boy, although a bit dim.

"And you'll recognize it….how?" I asked and he responded with a what-a-jerk-I-am look.

"How about….," he said with mock seriousness, "we get them <u>together</u>?"

"Sounds like a plan," I answered with not-so-subtle sarcasm. So, I got up and we walked together to the stairs. As we were nearing them, Craig reached out and put his arm around my shoulder. Now, <u>this</u> was interesting! OK, Molly, I thought, how do you want to react to this? Was this OK with me? Or not? Did I want this? Or didn't I? Does one said something? Or not? Somebody, PLEASE, I thought, give me the rule book! Mom never talked to me about this moment and, while I may have thought about it in the someday category, I never pictured it happening in the midst of some meaningless keg party. The half-a-buzz I had on also wasn't helping.

My internal romantic crisis must have mutated to my shoulder, or my face, or something, because he quickly slipped his arm back off. I suspect I probably flinched and tightened my back enough to send some kind of unconscious message. Then I was trying to decide if I should say anything, apologize, tell him it was OK, tell him to keep his damn hands off of me, or SOMETHING! The truth was that I was not at all sure I wanted him to stop, and not at all sure I wanted him to continue.

"Sorry," he said quietly.

"Don't worry about it." Oh, <u>good</u>, Molly, that was <u>real</u> deep, <u>real</u> insightful! I'm sure he understood <u>everything</u> then. Instantly, we were back in awkward mode. He had the nerve to put his hand on my shoulder. Big, fat, hairy damn deal! Jeez, that was a crime, wasn't it?

We trotted up and got the coats, trading nervous smiles, and headed back down stairs. When we were back on the main floor I asked him to hold up a minute. He nodded OK and I ran back into the kitchen, grabbed a pitcher and a cup, and poured down two quick ones. It rushed to my head as I bumped my buzz back up a notch or two. "I'm ready now," I announced as I threw on my coat, opened the door and stepped out onto the front porch with Craig following.

The cold air was an attention-getter after sitting in the hot party air, and our breath shone and floated like silver smoke in the glare of the porch light. The quiet of the dark street was lush and welcome after the clatter and chatter of the party, and it felt like stepping out of a cartoon frame and into a row boat on a quiet lake. No noise, just the soft sound of the crisp breeze blowing through the almost barren branches of the silhouetted trees. We stood there for a few moments, acclimating to the change, letting our senses adjust to the dark, the quiet, and the cold, and fumbling with small talk.

After a moment or two, as we adjusted to this odd setting, Craig asked with another stupid smile for the second time in one evening, "SO, uh, do you come here often?"

I laughed, feeling increasingly less anxious. "As infrequently as possible," I answered. "This is my first and, uh, most likely, my last visit to the People's Park. Ain't no people here!"

"No people with any brains, anyway," he noted.

"Speak for yourself!" I cautioned, trying to maintain my best sense of phony indignation.

"Whose idea was it in the first place?" he inquired with mocked shock.

"Who agreed with the idea in the second place?" I retorted quickly.

"OK, OK. How about if we both just agree that it was a brilliant although eccentric idea conceived by two people who'd rather be cold than crowded? How about that, huh? Does that get us both of the 'stupid hook' if we freeze to death out here?"

"Sounds like a plan, Craig, sounds like a plan." We were both laughing as Craig put his arm around me once again and this time, I didn't flinch. It was initially a funny feeling both emotionally and physically to have somebody outside of family holding you but, in short order, his arm adjusted to the shape of my shoulder as we both shifted until it felt comfortable. I leaned against him a bit as it seemed like we needed to send each other signals about what's all right, what's working. We were making it up as we went along, and it was both exciting and confusing at the same time. He started to rub my arm and shoulder with his hand, and it made a soft, whistling sound on the material of my winter coat. He squeezed my shoulder a bit more and as I turned to him in a natural reaction to the sensation, he kissed me.

This was it. The real deal. The first kiss. The moment you've wondered about since that time in childhood when it comes to you that someday, somewhere, you could actually be involved in this strange ritual. The age when you were past the point where the mere concept was revolting. ("Ugh, I'll never kiss a boy like that!"). When kids stopped teasing each other with jingles like "Molly and Craig, up in a tree / Kay-eye-ess-ess- eye-en-gee!" Since then, there had been internal speculation about the event, about how it might feel, and what makes it such a big deal. How you would do it? Well, not literally how you would do it, as it's obvious how you do it. But, you know...how do you do it? Who starts it? How long? Could you practice? No more thinking about it then. It was happening!

My first thoughts? Big whoop! What was all the fuss about? It didn't feel like much, actually a bit strange. Frankly, I thought about how damn cold his lips were and wondered if mine were that frosty. I felt extremely self-conscious, and just wondered if I was doing it right (whatever the hell right was.) He put his arms around me and squeezed, so I put mine around him and squeezed back. We kissed again, and again, and after a few more tries, I think we were getting the hang of it! His lips weren't cold anymore, and I knew mine weren't. We mutually worked out a rhythm that was smooth and comfortable, and I started to get a sense of why this kissing stuff was such a hit. I didn't realize what I had been missing!

We kept on kissing, and I sort of lost track of time (which, as may be noticed by now, isn't an unusual occurrence for me). However, I had a gradual transformation back to the here and now as the mercury kept dipping. Romantic moment though it was, I was freezing! I broke the lip-lock and broke the news. "Hey, Craig, I hate to ruin the mood, but I'm cold."

To my surprise, Craig didn't look disappointed. He looked relieved! "Yeah, I gotta agree with you. It's frigid out here! Wanna go back?"

By now, my teeth were chattering. "I think so! Let's go, I'm losing the feeling in my toes!"

We hustled back to the party trying to work up some warmth by walking quickly, but to no avail. Fortunately, we didn't get lost, which was a minor miracle considering the random route we had taken. We just retraced some of our frozen footsteps back. Actually, it was kind of fun, and we were giggling and chattering all at the same time while we walked. "Thank God!" Craig exclaimed, "we're saved!" as the house emerged from the frosty streetlights as we turned a corner. We ran the rest of the way, down the street, up the porch steps, and into the front door. We collapsed against the door after we slammed it shut, laughing and reeling from the pleasant shock of warm air that makes your skin feel prickly, tingly, and alive.

The party had thinned out some since we left, but the noise level was still at the max. We returned to the couch we had left, which was luckily unoccupied. Craig snatched us a pitcher of beer and some cups and we downed a couple, which in retrospect was not a good idea given our fatigue from the earlier drinking, the emotion, the walk, and the weather. I knew I should have just gone home, but I didn't want the evening to end. Instead, I ended up with a head swimming from the suds and a realization that I was in no shape to drive home. I was certainly not an experienced drinker or driver, and I was dizzy and disoriented. "Look, Craig, I can't drive home like this," I said. "I've got to sober up."

"Hey, that's OK. I can give you a ride."

What a Boy Scout! "Oh, really? How?"

"I've got a car. I live kinda close to here but I can swing you over to your place and then come back. I'd hang around with you, I really would, but if I don't show home with the car, my parents will hang me. I'm on probation already. I'll be a permanent pedestrian."

"And, uh, what do I do with my mother's car?"

"Leave it here. You can get it tomorrow."

"There's the small problem of what I tell my mother when she asks why I'm being dropped off by some guy she's never met <u>and</u> without her car."

"Well, what are your choices? You can't drive the way you are now."

I had a situation on my hands, for sure. "I don't know, Craig. I think I'd be all right if I could just lay down for awhile."

Suddenly, Craig jumped up and said, "Hold on. Let me check something out for you."

"What?" I yelled as he disappeared, "What?"

"Just hold on, will ya?" he yelled back from another room. I sat there, realizing I didn't have a lot of options. After a few minutes, he reappeared. "Look," he said, "I talked to Jack. He said his parents aren't coming home tonight and they've got four bedrooms. You can sleep in one of the spare ones until you feel all right. There's a couple of kids crashing here already."

"I can't sleep here! What a wacky idea!"

"And why not?"

"I don't live here!"

"Would you prefer to die on the road home to where you do live?"

"Uh, good point. But, I'll feel weird!"

"For all of about two minutes before you fall asleep." I tried to think of convincing reasons why I shouldn't do this, but I was too foggy to debate. "I'll come back in the daylight and check on you if you want."

"I'm not a baby, Craig. I don't need to be checked on." I was starting to get irritable from the beer, the fatigue, and the logic box I was hemmed in.

"I'm just trying to be nice, Molly," he explained patiently. He was suprisingly gentle in the face of my crabbiness.

"It's not you, Craig. I'm just tired."

"I know, I know. Just go sleep it off."

I was too tired to continue the debate and besides, I knew he was right. "OK. I'll go lay down for awhile."

He smiled. "All right! Good choice."

I went and thanked Jack for the hospitality, and we both walked upstairs where we found a room that looked like it was set up for a little boy: car posters on the wall, HotWheels all over the floor, and interesting-looking Lego creations. I'd been carrying my coat around with me since we returned and I flung it on a chair in the room, along with my bag. "This'll do fine," I announced. I was sinking fast.

Ordinarily, this would be a high-tension situation - me alone in a bedroom with a boy who interests me. Actually, it could have been a "situation" if it happened several hours earlier, one I wasn't prepared to deal with. Now, however, it was feeling more platonic than romantic. "Good night," I said, and gave him a kiss that said "I'm tired, go away," although in the nicest way! He got the message.

"Good night. I'll check on you in the morning."

"No. Look, why don't you just give me a call? My number's in the book under my mother's name, Margaret Wooding."

"OK, I'll call you then."

"OK. Now, go!"

"Bye," he said, kissed me quickly, and left. I flopped down on the bed, and there was no danger of doing the "Three Bears" routine then. Any bed would have been "just right!" including that one. I glanced at a clock on a dresser that read 12.02 a.m., and quickly faded away.

I don't know how long I was asleep. It's hard enough to distinguish reality from the sandman when you're coming to after a normal's night sleep. Like, when you take a nap after you get home from school and wake up a couple of hours later, wondering what day it is, what time it is, and what planet you live on, thoroughly disoriented. It seemed like an impossible task in a dark room in a strange house in the middle of the night at some god-awful hour. But there I was, laying there, getting this uncomfortable feeling while still sleeping, or at least while still less than conscious. In the distance I heard the noise of the party, which was apparently still going strong, but the sounds were fuzzy and confusing, out of place. The uncomfortable feeling grew, as did my awareness and I slowly began to realize that I wasn't alone. I also realized that someone was touching me. Touching me! Somebody's hand was on my stomach, and my shirt was unbuttoned! My eyes flashed open, and I was staring at some guy I'd never seen before, or at least didn't recognize. Holy shit! He was laying next to me, and my blouse was damn near off!

"Who the hell are you?" I yelled, and moved to get up. "What are you doing?" I didn't recognize the guy at all, although he probably was at the party. He had brown hair shaved on the bottom but long and straight on the top, kind of in a bowl cut, and it half-covered his eyes as he was laying there.

This guy smiled at me! "Hi," he said, and wrapped his arm around my waist, holding me down. His breath stunk with the smell of stale beer and cigarettes. He was leaning with his head resting on his other hand and as I continued to struggle to get up, he slipped that arm around my back and wrapped the fingers of his hand on my neck. He pushed himself up and over me, and then he was holding me down with the weight of his body and the one arm over my neck. His other hand was moving up my chest, and he was grabbing my breasts, rubbing them, and tugging at my bra, trying to pull it off.

"Get the hell off of me!" I croaked, and it was hard to get any volume because of the weight on me. "Get off!" I struggled to get up, to move, to do something. My heart was beating so fast, I was hyperventilating and drowning in terror. As I struggled, he put his forearm across my neck and pressed. I was choking, struggling to breath! He brought his face down close to mine, right next to me, and the sickening smell was even stronger. His brown eyes were bloodshot and the pupils dilated, and I could see the excitement in them.

"Shut up," he whispered, and pressed even harder. "Shut the <u>fuck</u> up!" I tried to swing my arms, and he reached and pinned them behind me, holding me at the wrists with one of his hands. I was now completely immobilized, and his free hand was fondling me, with my bra now half pulled off. He reached down with his free hand and started to stick his hand down the front of my jeans. As he was doing so, he took his eyes off of mine, and his shoulder hovered close to my mouth. The pressure on my shoulders lessened as his arm moved and he shifted his weight to reach down, and I lurched up, latched my teeth onto the top of his arm, and I bit down, hard, tasting the cotton of his shirt. "Ouh!" he yelled, and he flipped off of me and off the bed, half-falling, half-scrambling. He was kind of sitting on the floor on the side of the bed in this awkward position, rubbing and looking at his shoulder. He pulled up the sleeve on his shirt to check his wound, and I damn near launched myself right off the bed into a standing position, and ran out the door, grabbing my coat and bag from the chair as I went.

The overhead light in the hallway flooded my eyes like a flashbulb as I scrambled out the bedroom door. My blouse was barely draped over on my shoulders and I tugged at my bra to straighten it out as I ran down the hall, my fingers trembling. I damn near tumbled down the steps in my panic as I threw my coat on while descending, and I caught myself just before I fell. My legs were buckling beneath me. I could hear the sound of music and people talking and laughing from different rooms, and I fought the urge to throw up. My only focus was the front door and getting out of it, but it was kind of like one of those nightmares where you can see safety in the distance but can't get to it, no matter how hard you run, and where you try to scream for help, but no sound will come out.

In this nightmare, though, I finally made it to the door, flung it open, and ran out, stumbling down the porch stairs and down the walk. I was running with my coat and shirt open and flapping, and the cold air swirled around my stomach and chest as I ran. I made it to my car, pulled open the door with such force that it hurt my shoulder, and jumped in, banging my ribs on the steering wheel. I sat there in the dark and the cold, hyperventilating, watching as my breath came out in short, gray bursts in the cold, like a little locomotive. I realized my shirt was open and started to fumble with the buttons, getting one or two fastened but no more, as I was shaking too hard. I wanted to run out the door and down the street. I wanted to disappear forever. I wanted to not be. I wanted to die.

I sat there and realized that I was still trapped. I couldn't drive because I was too panicked, but I felt like the walls of the car would compress and crush me. I looked into the rearview mirror, and gazed hard at myself. Who the hell was this? What had this face got to do with me? Short, blonde hair, a few freckles, bloodshot blue eyes, swollen from trying not to cry. Alien! I watched my mouth move with little, quick movements from my panicky breathing, fogging the mirror a little if I moved close. I turned away, it made me sick! Had to do something, had to make it stop! I eyed the steering wheel and smacked my forehead on it. It made a curious, dull sound when I made contact, and the pain shot through my head like a small explosion. I banged it over and over until I was dizzy from the combination of the pain and the rapid head movements, stopping only when I felt like I'd pass out. Suddenly, exhaustion settled in. Softly, I started to cry, and as I did, it was as if I opened the gate to the all the frustration, loneliness, and sadness locked inside. I cried and cried, sobbed and heaved, and cried and cried. The tears were like a poison pouring out from somewhere deep inside, and it hurt! Goddammit, it hurt! Didn't anybody see? <u>Why</u> didn't anybody see? Why was I so alone? What was I going to do? What was I going to do? <u>Somebody</u>, please, please, help me! I couldn't go on like this, I couldn't go on. I <u>hated</u> myself.

There was a knock on the door on the car door, and I jumped from the startle. I sucked in the sobs and croaked, "Go away!"

"Are you OK?" a girl's voice asked with concern, looking in the car window at me.

"Fine." Yeah, <u>right</u>!

"Are you sure?" I guess I was less than convincing.

"<u>Yes</u>, I'm sure! Go away!" There was no response, and after awhile she just shrugged her shoulders and walked away. I put my face in my hands to make it darker, and then started to moan and rock, back and forth, moan and rock, back and forth. Moaning and rocking. Moaning. And rocking. Moaning. And rocking. I slipped into the time warp again, for how long I have no idea, and when I returned, I had no clue what time it was. I was drained, empty, exhausted, and numb. (And my head hurt!) The objects in the car, like the dashboard, steering wheel, the seat, were ghostly silhouettes as I sat in the dark. You know, sitting there, I found out after experimentation that no matter what you do it's pretty much impossible to make it completely dark, completely black. Try as you might, some light seeps through, and eventually you can make out forms and shapes. You can run, but you really can't hide. Goddamn life finds you.

OK, Molly, what now? I couldn't spend the rest of my life, pitiful though it was, sitting in this car. I turned on the interior light and checked out my face in the rearview mirror. I looked like six miles of rough road, with bruises on my forehead, eyes that were almost swollen shut from crying, and hair sticking up all over the place from running my tear-soaked fingers through it. What little eye make-up I did use was smeared from the tears. I wiped my face with a tissue in my purse, and ran a comb I found through my hair. I was tired and wired from the drinking, the emotion, and the fact that is had to be the middle of the damn night. I sat quietly in the dark.

The middle of the night has always been spooky to me, which is why I think it's my favorite time of day, but in the cold it's even more interesting. The chill, combined with the dark, seems to put a dome over the land that distant sounds can't penetrate and sounds closer to you seem unable to escape. In the dark, the quiet, and the cold, you become acutely self-aware because there isn't much to distract. As I sat there, it felt like every house was watching me, even though I knew it was not likely that anyone was awake. In the absence of people, inanimate objects on the street, like porches, trees, street lamps, and yard ornaments seemed to come alive, whispering "What are you doing up at this hour?" and "Why aren't you home asleep?" and "What are you doing in our neighborhood?" I cleared my throat and it sounded like thunder. I put the key in the ignition, turned it, and started the car.

Where was I going to go? Where did I belong? If I could have, I'd have pointed the car at the horizon and just driven away, far away, until the hollow, aching feeling in the pit of my stomach went away. I'd have driven until I reached a place where I'd really be a stranger instead of just feeling like one. I'd have driven until I fell off the end of the earth and just drifted away, into space, floating until I turned into a satellite that slowly orbited the earth, where I could look down on the meaningless below with an amused smile, grateful that I was above it all, living safe and isolated in the dark, still void of celestial nothingness. Maybe then I could believe in heaven. Maybe then I could believe in something. Instead, my choices were pretty limited. Home. That was about it.

So, I pulled the car out onto the street and drove home, making the required lefts and rights at the required times, stopping at the stop signs and red lights as needed, speeding up and slowing down, going through the motions in another pointless trip in my pointless life. I pulled into the driveway, turned off the ignition and the lights, and gazed in the early morning darkness at my "home." If I didn't feel so damn bad, I think the word would have made me break out with laughter. Instead, it just made me sad. I slithered into the house with the utmost stealth, as a meeting with my mother then would have been the end of me. I wasn't even supposed to be there, I was supposed to be spending the night with "friends" (another oxymoron). I crept into my room, tossed my coat, slipped off my shoes, and laid down softly on my bed. I gazed up again at that old familiar ceiling with that old familiar feeling. Me, the ceiling, and my aloneness. Now, I was home.

CHAPTER 4

Sleep was good. I was finding it increasingly hard to come by, but when I found it, I liked it. It was a window in the wall of my life that I could pry open and slide through, a space where my mind finally shut the hell up. Sometimes the nightmares were a problem, but that which I dreamed often paled in comparison to that which I lived, at least in terms of how I perceived it. Horror, after all, is a very subjective experience, which explains why some people laugh at scary movies while others cry at *Bambi*. I've always fit the latter category. I've had the eerie feeling that I'm in the sights of a high-powered rifle for awhile myself.

I don't know when or how it happened, but I did doze off laying there. I awakened on that brief, fleeting island in time where you have no immediate memory of how you felt or what happened the night before, where you think anything's possible that day, where all the options are open, and where the slate seems clean. This hallucination only lasts for seconds, though, before you remember, before the whole damn past comes crashing back, and there you are. Same nobody you were the day before. It's like being given the same bad news every day except each time seems like the first.

This day, however, was uniquely awful. Mom was gone, which wasn't unusual on Saturday because she'd slip out to grocery-shop, pick up various things we needed, or run other errands. She'd generally let me sleep as she had learned through repeated trials that efforts to get me up were usually going to be unsuccessful. She must not have made much of the fact that I was home when I was supposed to be sleeping over. It was almost noon.

I felt like hell and, when I looked in my bedroom mirror, I found out I looked like it, too. The bruises on my forehead were swollen, angry and multicolored, and my eyes didn't look great, either, from the drinking and the crying. My hair was jutting out here and there in some unique formations. I looked like the ultimate punker. My head hurt, both inside and outside, and I was sore all over. I was also quite fond of that morning mouthful of God-knows-what. I stared at myself in the mirror and saw the same face I stared at last night. In some ways, this face seemed more appropriate. Felt like shit, looked like shit.

After downing a couple of aspirins, I flossed, brushed my teeth and resisted the temptation to swallow the mouthwash as I swirled it around. I turned on the shower, adjusted the water until it was too hot to keep my hand under it for more than a few seconds, and then dialed it back just a tad. Stepping into the steaming stream, I felt the sting of the scalding water, and I welcomed the shock. I stood there letting the countless beads bounce off my body and, when I gradually grew accustomed to the water temperature, I'd reach down and crank it up a tad. Hurting myself seemed to be my only way of confirming that I existed, and there are countless ways to do it when you start looking for them. Besides, cleanliness is next to godliness, or some such nonsense as that. That's either good news for soap sales or bad news for religion, depending on your point of view.

I did what I could with my hair, and put a cold washcloth over my eyes for a few minutes to try to get the swelling down. I played with the make-up for awhile, trying to cover the bruise on my forehead with only limited success. I shuffled into my mother's bedroom in my underwear, stood a few feet back from her full length mirror, assessed my remedial efforts, and my only thought was, "Who the hell is this?" I gazed at me. About five foot, six inches tall and 120 lbs., last I checked. Blondish hair cut short, as I was increasingly less-and-less interested in screwing around with it. Hips that were too small and a chest that was, too. I've been told I have nice long legs, but they looked fat to me. I kind of looked like a young boy who was having a gender-identity crisis. <u>Nothing</u> seemed to fit. I was like one of those push-out cardboard dolls that you can assemble using pieces from all kinds of different models. You know, where you stick the blonde's head with the brunette's body and the redhead's arms and legs, trying to make it as silly as you can. As I looked in the mirror, it seemed like the ultimate state of silliness had been achieved. None of the pieces belonged. I was a freak.

I went back to my room and dressed in my usual psuedo-skater look: baggy pants, sweatshirt, and sneakers. (I generally tried to avoid either a "she" look or a "he" look. I think I was in search of an "it" look.) As I slid down the steps, I quickly assessed my interest in breakfast, decided I had none, and went into the living room where I tossed a CD on the stereo and flopped on the couch. My musical selections had always been eclectic and my choices ranged from heavy metal to classical vocalists, all sharing a common thread of feeling miserable. It seemed sort of strange to pick music to match a mood, rather than choosing something that could improve it, but misery loves company, especially if you don't have to talk to it. Today's selection? Nine Inch Nails. How appropriate.

As the tunes were helping me maintain that super-shitty feeling, Mom strolled in the door and I quickly ratcheted down the volume with the remote. "Listening to that garbage again?" Mom asked with her best disapproving stare.

"It's not Garbage, Mom. That's another group." Boy, I was witty.

She was looking at me with that what-are-you-talking-about look when she suddenly stopped dead in her tracks. "<u>What</u> happened to you?" she asked, staring at the knot on my forehead. I guess my cosmetics didn't cut it.

"Nothing, Mom, don't worry about it." Oh, yeah, <u>that's</u> creative, that'll work real well!

"What do you mean 'Don't worry about it'? That's one nasty looking bump on your head. Besides, why are you home? You told me you were staying over at Jasmine's house."

Amazing, but I wasn't prepared with an explanation for last night, despite knowing at some level that I was going to be facing that moment of untruth. "I didn't feel real good so I decided to come home." Couldn't call me a liar.

"I'll bet you didn't feel good judging by that bruise. How did that happen?" By the seriousness of her expression, I knew I'd better be convincing.

"We were horsing around in Jasmine's bedroom and I slipped and hit my head on the edge of her dresser."

"Why didn't you call me, or wake me up when you got home? That looks like it hurts." If she only knew.

"I didn't want to bother you."

"Molly, don't be ridiculous! If you're hurt, I want to know about it! What if it was serious?" It was, Mom, it was.

"It was <u>nothing</u>, Mom. Nothing. <u>Really</u>. Don't make a big deal out of it."

"Get used to it, Molly. That's what mothers do. They make big deals out of things."

"Well, then, your mother membership must be in good standing,"

"Excellent, excellent. By the way, you had a phone call earlier when you were sleeping."

"Really? Who?"

"It was a boy, a boy named Craig. Who's he? I don't think I've ever met him or heard you talk about anybody with that name." I almost gasped out loud. Was she watching me?

"He's nobody, Mom, just a kid from school." I had forgotten that he might call. I had also not given any thought to how I'd explain meeting him, and any off-the-cuff explanation seemed way too fraught with the potential for screwing up the details.

I got that look again! "Then what's he calling about?"

Think quick! "We're in the same math class, Mom. We sit close and he sometimes asks me about the homework. I have no clue why he called but I'm guessing it has something to do with that." I snuck a glance in her direction and she was shuffling around the kitchen, putting groceries away, not looking at me. Thank God!

"I don't remember seeing him around. Well, anyway, I told him I'd give you the message that he called. He didn't want to leave his phone number; he said he'd try later."

"OK, thanks, Mom." My heart was throbbing like a finger hit with a hammer and I felt like I was wearing a "MOLLY IS LYING THROUGH HER TEETH!" sign around my neck.

"He sounded nice enough. Did you eat something for breakfast?"

"Yeah, Mom, I had some cereal." Yesterday.

"Are you full?"

Full? Oh, yeah, I'm full of it, up to my ears. "<u>Yes</u>, Mom! I'm fine!"

"OK, OK! Don't get testy! Boy, you're crabby today." Sometimes, it's the inadvertent conversations that are <u>so</u> ironic. Just as I was trying to envision the next sardonic twist this talk could take, the phone in the kitchen rang! I almost had a freaking heart attack with each ring before Mom answered, asked the caller to hold on, and announced, "Molly, it's for you. It's Jennifer." I started breathing again.

"I'll take it in my room, Mom," I said as I ran and grabbed the cordless phone in the hallway, and bolted into my bedroom. "I got it, Mom," I yelled as I clicked the phone on, and she hung up. "Hello?"

"Hey, how the hell are you?" Jennifer asked in an excited way. "What happened after I left last night?"

"Never mind. Nothing. How's Suzanne?" I inquired, hoping to change the subject.

"Still asleep, last I checked. I called her house a little while ago and her sister told me she wasn't up yet. I wouldn't be surprised if we don't hear from her for the rest of the weekend. She was <u>totally</u> baked last night. I drove her home and she made it up to her front door. She was stumbling in last I saw her. I hope she was able to make it to her bedroom without barfing, or something."

"Me, too."

"How are you feeling?"

Oh, brother! "Less than great."

"Why? How much longer did you stay? What did happen with, uh, what's his name?" I wasn't going to just slide around this, I could tell.

"Not much."

"Whadda ya mean, 'not much'? You two were looking like an item when we left. How'd you make out or, should I said, did you make out? C'mon, give me the gory details!"

Silence.

"Hey, are you still there?"

Silence.

"Molly, c'mon. Answer me."

"I'd rather not."

Her voice was registering concern. "Why? What's the matter? What happened?" "Nothing. Nothing happened." I suppose there were possible ways to get my neck out of this noose more gracefully, but my creative lying was not up to par at the moment. Jenn knew she was onto something. "Look, I'm coming over."

"The hell you are!"

"C'mon, Molly, something's wrong, and I want to know what's got you so upset." Mother Jennifer was on the mothering scent again, and I knew that it would be hard to lie my way out of this with her. She had a sixth sense that detected a friend hurting, and also had a strong Dudley DoRight complex that compelled her to try to fix whatever ailed you.

"<u>Nothing</u> happened. Besides, I can't go out."

"Why? Why can't you go out?" Did I detect skepticism?

"Because." Again, you've <u>got</u> to admire my creative power with lying. "OK, girl, I'll be over in a little while as soon as I talk Dad out of the car." Before I could protest, Jenn hung up the phone. Great! Now what? Did I want a friend to know? Did I want to tell her? If I did, what would I say? "Well, actually, Jenn, it was real romantic, up to the point where I was almost raped by some stranger. It made me feel <u>so</u> special. I felt <u>so</u> understood." How does one explain perhaps one of the most terrifying moments in my life? Better yet, how would I explain the bruise on my forehead? I could say that somebody hit me! No, that would be lying and I'm not only still pure, I'm honest, too. I was finding the awesome weight of sainthood difficult to bear. In any event, I figured that my internal dialogue was essentially a waste of time as Jenn was on her way over, whether I wanted it or not, so I went to let Mom know she was coming over.

As I made my way back to the kitchen, the phone rang. Mom answered with the usual greetings, said "It's for you," and handed me the phone. I figured it was Jennifer calling to announce a change of heart, or maybe the absence of wheels, so I said "Hello" with a rush of relief, thinking I was to be spared the telling vs. not telling dilemma. I heard "Hi, Molly" from a male voice that I didn't immediately recognize, so I asked, "Who's this?", hoping against hope. A brief moment of silence and then I heard, "It's Craig."

I did not know what to do. I did not know what to say. If I cut the call real short, I would have had some big explaining to do to Mom. I assumed Mom recognized the voice from the previous phone call, so she was expecting me to shoot the shit about Math homework with a classmate. Calling on my deepest powers of creativity, I answered "Yeah?"

"Hey, how are you? It's good to hear your voice. Did you make it home OK last night?" He had no idea what a minefield he was stepping into.

"Yeah, I did. How about you?" How was I supposed to give him a summary of being attacked? I was dying from the shame. What was I supposed to talk about with him now? Geez, it was really special last night, right up to the point where I was almost raped? I don't think so. I've also got Mom. She's trying hard to not look like she's listening which only makes it all the more apparent that she is.

"I was a bit late, but no big deal. It was worth it to meet you. I really had a good time. I was wondering if you'd like to go out with me tonight someplace. Catch a movie or something. I can swing by and pick you up."

I felt bad. He had no idea what happened, and was probably expecting to start where we left off. I had no idea what to say, or if I wanted to say anything. I hadn't prepared for the rest of my life. "I don't know, Craig." I could tell by the extended silence after this comment that he wasn't prepared for that, and I couldn't blame him. "Could you call me later?" I needed some time to think.

"Sure," he said, sounding a bit puzzled. "What'll be a good time?"

Another question! I couldn't plan, I couldn't see past the next minute. "I don't know. Just give it a try later."

Again, the silence. "OK. I'll call you later."

I felt guilty, but I just couldn't handle it. "OK, bye," and I hung up the phone.

"So, what did he want?" Mom asked, probing.

"Uh, <u>math</u> stuff, Mom. Duh?"

"Don't be disrespectful," Mom snorted, and walked away. Nothing like a little impudence to squelch a parent-child conversation. As she rounded the corner out of the kitchen, I started to breath normally again. The pressure of this performance was exhausting, and I was weak in the knees from the stress. The call had put me on the spot with

Mom, and brought me back big time to the events of the previous night. Somehow, I couldn't get over the feeling that I deserved what had happened. I was doing a big case of the "if onlys"; if only I hadn't gone, if only I hadn't drank, if only I left with Craig, and so on. There was no end to them, I just kept coming up with different combinations. I also identified with the pitiful actress in that series of horror movies who was always too stupid to get away from the guy, no matter how many times he tried to kill her. Sometimes, it gets real difficult to have any empathy or sympathy for the victim when she seems totally spineless. I guess that's one of the reasons I was having a hard time feeling any for myself. I made her look downright assertive. Some victims deserve what they get. I know I did.

Just in time, two bright, moving lights pierced the kitchen curtains, and I peeked out and spotted Jenn's car. I waved to let her know I saw her and yelled, "Mom, I'm going out with Jenn. I won't be out late."

"Where are you going?" she asked.

"Nowhere, Mom." Wasn't <u>that</u> the truth? There's that irony again. Actually, irony is all around you when you start looking for it, and sometimes even when you're not.

"OK, don't be late."

"Don't worry, Mom." No, change that. Worry, Mom, worry.

I grabbed my coat, ran out the door, and jumped in Jenn's car. "Hey, Jenn."

"Hey, yourself. I thought you couldn't go out."

"Actually, I had that backwards. I couldn't stay."

Jennifer was talking to me over her shoulder as she looked back while pulling out of the driveway. "Spill the beans, girlfriend. The tension's killing me."

"C'mon, let's just get away from here first." I needed some miles between me and home. Truth be told, I needed some miles between me and me, but it's a bitch arranging transportation for that trip. "Let's just drive around." In adolescence, it seems to me that many, many miles are covered with no particular destination, no particular point. Or, perhaps, that is the point, to get away from instead of go to. So tonight, this drive was about much more than killing time. I was gagging on the sour taste of the symbolism.

We drove around, lefting, righting, going straight, cruising through neighborhoods we've passed through since we were born. But, you know, it's either curious or tragic that we drive by each other's homes, cruise by each other's lives, and generally don't give a second's thought to all the people inside. I gazed at the homes as we sailed by, and I wondered what was happening behind all those walls. Were those inside happy? Did they get along? Care for each other? Was there anyone who felt settled? Secure? Safe? Were there moms and dads in there who really, really, loved each other; who hugged and kissed in front of their kids in sloppy, romantic ways that embarrassed the kids while making them feel special to see it; who joked, smiled, and kidded with each other with a look between them that let the kids know that they were created as a living testimony to that love and not just to have perky props for the holiday family photos; who waited up at night for the kids to come home on the weekends, no matter how late it was, instead of leaving a note on a table and going to bed? And how about the kids? Were there children in those houses who knew that, no matter what, this was the one place you could count on to be there in all the ways you needed it, when you needed it? Where home was pretty much an answer rather than an unfathomable question?

"Hello? Earth to Molly."

La-la land; I was visiting again. "Sorry," I answered truthfully. "Didn't mean to zone out on you."

"Well, you did. Again." Jennifer is an interesting person. Her personality is a combination of dreamer and realist that helps her see both the stars and the earth beneath her feet. With her small stature, long, dark hair and soft, gentle-looking face, one could make the big mistake of taking her for granted. I've seen others make that assumption on several occasions, only to find out that the arrows of Jenn's words rarely missed their mark. She was accomplished at verbal archery. She also tended to see right through others' facades, and her frankness and honesty in such situations often left others wondering if they'd been complimented or dissected. Jenn called 'em like she saw 'em, and you either admired that or feared it. I was of the former persuasion. She was sort of my alter-ego, and I was envious of her self-assurance. "So, what's the deal? What the hell happened?"

"Hey, it was just one of those things."

She shot a Jenn-glance at me. "What the hell does <u>that</u> mean?"

"Look, Jenn. This isn't easy. It's been a tough couple of days. <u>Please</u>, spare me the third-degree. If I'm going to talk about this, I need you to listen, not criticize me. I got enough goddamn people telling me what I do wrong already!" Pretty spirited stuff for a wimp.

"I'm sorry, I'm sorry. I'll try. Just calm down, all right? Calm down."

"OK, OK."

We drove some more. "So?" She was stepping gingerly.

I looked at her, and thought about it, about telling her, that is. So I thought about it, and how to start. I though about it, and how to explain how I felt. I thought about it, and tried to understand why. While I was doing all this figuring, I started to cry, and I felt that old familiar panic coming on.

Jenn looked at me with this shocked look. "Molly, <u>what's</u> the matter? What happened?"

I was crying, and crying, and crying. "I can't, Jenn," I sobbed. "I can't." At that moment, I knew this was going to be a pattern. Some problems were too big to put into words. Some emotions were too confusing to translate. Some thoughts were too scary to recall. And this problem, these emotions, these thoughts were bigger, and more confusing, and scarier than any I'd ever experienced. "I can't."

Jennifer pulled the car to the side of the road and stared at me. "OK, Molly," she said consolingly, "OK. You don't have to if you don't want to."

"Jennifer," I sobbed, "you <u>don't</u> understand. I can't."

"It's all right, Molly. It's all right. You don't have to." I thought she understood, or at least recognized that she might have been opening a box whose contents she couldn't contain. She pulled out onto the street, and we drove, and drove, and drove some more. And I cried, and cried, and cried some more.

CHAPTER 5

Another night. Another trip into abyss. The dreams were weirder, more upsetting, more specific, many starring a brown-haired boy with bowl-cut hair and me. I didn't feel like I slept, but I must have, given the nightmare hangover I was having. All the bad effects, none of the good. It was about noon, and while I could have gotten up earlier as I was wide awake, I refused to rise, choosing instead to lay there, staring at the ceiling again. It was late when I returned last night, real late, and I was exhausted, but whatever sleep I was getting couldn't be especially deep as I was wired for sound. So, I laid there, somewhat to try to get some rest, somewhat out of stubbornness, but mostly to avoid it all, to put it off, to stall. Morning was a bit hard to take, anyway, what with all the "seize-the-day" and "get-off-on-a-good-foot" bullshit my mom tried to sell.

There was a knock on my bedroom door, and Mom said in the loud-mother-behind-the-door voice, "C'mon, Molly, get up! It's the afternoon, already!" and rapped her knuckles on the door again, just for effect.

"All right, Mom, all right," I answered tiredly. "I'm getting up." With great effort, I dragged my legs over the side of the bed, left them there for awhile, then mustered up the momentum to sit up on the side of the bed. Going vertical must have suddenly shifted some of the precious bodily fluids because I felt dizzy and faint for a few seconds. I waited awhile for the feeling to pass, and then rose. I hauled myself across the room and out the door, figuring I'd let Mom have a viewing and then try to figure a way to go back to bed. I made my way down the stairs. I hadn't gotten into a coffee ritual yet, but today could be the start of a brand new bad habit.

I shuffled into the kitchen where my Mom was straightening up. My brother was gone to his job at a local supermarket where he put in some weekend hours. Church hadn't been a part of our Sunday ritual since we were little kids when our parents were still together. We still claimed the Roman Catholic faith, but if I recall some of the guidelines from my early years in religious education, attendance at services on Sunday was supposed to be the rule, not the exception. Oh, well, we did go on the major holidays. Part-time was better than no-time at all. I actually think the divorce resulted in a self-imposed family ex-communication. The faith was shaken. Badly.

"What time did you get in last night, Molly?"

"Late, Mom." I walked over to the counter, took out a coffee cup, and started to pour a cup. While I was doing it, Mom was staring at me, and at first I thought she was just a bit shocked by me taking the coffee. But, as I looked at her looking at me, I realized she was staring at the marginally healed cuts on my arm. Uh, oh! I forgot to put on a robe and I was there with only my nightgown, both arms fully exposed. Her jaw was dropping a foot!

"<u>What</u> happened to your <u>arm</u>?" she asked, "Where did those cuts come from?" Her eyes were wide, her look disbelieving. Damn!

"Oh, those?" I responded meekly. "It was an accident." I had no idea how I was going to explain this.

"What <u>kind</u> of accident? When? What happened?" She was borderline frantic. "Let me see your arm." I couldn't think of any way out. I held out my arm and she came over and took it in her hands, scoping out all the cuts. "Molly, these look like razor cuts! How did they get there?" I was clueless. I couldn't think of a thing. "I don't know, Mom."

She almost rose right up off the ground, almost levitated. "<u>What</u> do you <u>mean</u>, you don't know? Don't lie to me, Molly!" Her voice was going up in volume with each word. "How did this happen?"

"I don't know, Mom." What could I say? My creative lying streak was at an end. "<u>Don't</u> <u>lie</u> <u>to</u> <u>me</u>!" She was just about screaming, her face red and her eyes on fire. "<u>Don't</u> lie to me!"

"I don't know." I was busted.

"Get dressed," Mom commanded while putting dishes in the sink, slamming them in so the silverware bounced when the bowls hit bottom. "Get dressed <u>now</u>!"

"Why?" I asked in a whiny voice, "What for?"

Mom gazed straight at me, her blue eyes flashing. "You're going to a walk-in so a doctor can check those cuts. Get <u>dressed</u>!"

I didn't want to do this, but I didn't know what else I could do. I had never seen Mom so upset, and I knew she wasn't going to let up. I went upstairs and started to dress. Actually, what surprised me the most about the whole exchange was how blasé I was feeling about it. I should have been panicked now, but I wasn't. My emotions made no sense anymore. Nothing made sense any more. Why should this be any different? I was strangely calm. I reached under my bed for my "cutting stash" and took out the razor. I sat on the edge of my bed, and pulled my nightgown up over my knees. I placed my hand over left thigh to hold the skin steady, and made four quick, short cuts on the inside of my thigh, high up. I was careful to not cut too deep, because I certainly couldn't deal with a lot of blood right then. I just needed the pain. It wasn't much, but it helped. No muss, not much fuss.

I came downstairs, dressed, and Mom was there waiting for me, pacing the floor. "You ready?" she asked impatiently.

"Yes," I answered blandly.

"Then get in the car."

We went outside, got in the car, and drove away from the house. The trip to the walk-in clinic in our neighborhood was a strained one, and Mom basically didn't talk to me the whole trip. She was breathing fairly heavy, and from the look on her face, trying hard not to put the pedal to the metal as she drove. While it was uncomfortable, it was better than trying to make conversation, <u>especially</u> now. We pulled into the parking lot of the walk-in, the "Associates in Medicine" (kinda sounded like a cult). Up the walk we walked, entered a waiting area and waited after Mom signed me in at the reception desk. I had been here before for some minor emergencies, like falls and cuts. How ironic! I'd fallen, and couldn't get up, and I was bleeding, both inside and outside, both literally and figuratively.

The place was moderately busy, and we waited about a half-hour or so leafing through magazines, looking at pictures while blind, reading while emotionally dyslexic. Funny, but I was surrounded mostly by aging issues of "People" magazine. I almost laughed out loud. So, <u>that's</u> where they were hiding! All the perky, happy people doing perky, happy things that don't amount to a stash of shit. What's the point? Is this what we're all supposed to strive for? To attend some mindless, self-affirming function wearing formal dresses with more cleavage than coverage while some tuxedoed stooge hangs on our arm, waving at some perfect stranger with a camera so we can be viewed by millions of perfect strangers who can look at us and drool, "Boy, I wish I was them"? OK. At least I know the goal.

"MOLLY MITCHELL." The receptionist called out the names like you were next for the executioner. "C'mon, Molly," Mom said and rose. I got up to follow, and I was somewhat puzzled about how much I didn't give a damn about this. I should have been freaked, but I wasn't. We walked into a hallway following this woman, and she gestured to one of the examining rooms. "The doctor will see you in here. She'll be along shortly," she said, and we walked in. I don't know why, but every time I'm in one of these places, I think of a Marx brothers routine I once saw where Dr. Groucho kept going in and out of the rooms, doors opening and shutting, patients scurrying around, and

Groucho's cigar dangling from his mouth the whole time as he's chasing this nurse with huge hooters. I don't think he'd be chasing the woman who led us in.

Seating arrangements were always a puzzle in these examining rooms. There was like one seat and an examining table. While waiting, what's the proper protocol? Should I, the "patient," sit on the table? It kind of looked like a meat counter at the butchers with the addition of a pillow of sorts. They even had the butcher's paper that they pull down over the table for each new "kill." Obviously, Mom shouldn't have sat there. Indeed, she'd already planted herself on the chair. The doctor wasn't going to sit there. That left me, so I hopped up and sat on the edge. Mom flipped through some of the (what else?) "People" magazines that were in a rack by the chair that send the clear message that you can plan on being here for awhile. Those who feel they're home free when they get into one of these rooms are deluding themselves. Same old shit, different scene. The movement merely gives one the illusion of progress. We were still cattle in a pen. I stared out the small window that was in the room, and noticed that there was a depressing mixture of flurries, sleet, and rain falling down outside. Perfect!

A nurse came in shortly and told us she needed to do an update on height, weight, blood pressure, etc. She directed me to the various scales, but when she went to take my blood pressure, I made a point of giving her my cut-free arm. No need to alarm the poor girl. With measurements measured, she left, and again we waited.

Time in these places is distorted, with a minute lasting a lifetime. You listen to the opening and closing of doors in the hallway, and the shuffling of feet, and you wonder, us next? But, then you hear a door open and close somewhere else in the hall. Nope, apparently not.

After about a day, or two, or three, there was a knock on the door. What were we going to say? Don't come in? Who's there? Protocol again. This woman in a lab coat came in, said "Hello, I'm Dr. Edelstein" to Mom, and then "Hello" to me. She was flipping through a chart that had God-knows-what on it. She looked at it with a bit of a puzzled look, and then apparently decided to get it straight from the horse's mouth (whatever that means). "So, what can I do for you today?" Once again, I resisted the urge to laugh out loud at the possible answers that popped into my mind, each of which would only dig my hole deeper.

There was a brief period of silence while it was informally decided who would speak first. I'd already made up my mind. It wasn't gonna be me! So, Mom caved in first. "Well, Doctor, Molly has some cuts on her arm that I found out about today, and I wanted to have them checked to make sure she's OK." I said to myself, don't laugh, Molly, don't laugh!

She turned and looked at me. "All right, Molly, lets see what we've got." I love the collective "we". Whadda ya mean, "we"? "Where are these cuts?"

"They're on her arm, Doctor," Mom offered, and I guess she figured out I wasn't likely to be the most responsive patient. Besides, there's that awkward stage that comes when you're no longer a little kid when Mom or Dad gave all the answers, but not quite old enough for everyone to assume you'll answer for yourself. The doctor kept shifting her view from me to Mom and back, trying to be politically correct.

"OK, Molly, pull up your sleeve and let me see." I held out the suspect limb and pulled the sleeve of the sweatshirt up, and she lightly held my arm in her hands and looked. I have to hand it to the woman, she was pretty casual and cool about it. "These are some nasty looking cuts, Molly," and she looked at me. "Do you have any others?" I suspected that the jig was up.

Again, Mom answered. "Not that I'm aware of, Doctor." She looked at Mom, and then back at me. "Are there, Molly?" The eye contact was more direct now, more serious.

"No," I said with all the conviction I could muster, which wasn't a whole lot. She kind of paused, and I think she was trying to figure out what to do, or where to go with this.

"How did these happen?" she finally asked.

"I don't know." Now, I was aware that it made absolutely no sense to give this answer. I knew there was absolutely no way something like this could happen without me being aware of it. I just didn't give a good goddamn. Deal with it!

"These look like they were made with a razor, or some other sharp, bladed instrument. Were they, Molly?"

"I already told you. I don't know." I showed the proper degree of irritation to keep the illusion alive, although I didn't think it was doing any damn good at all.

Silence again for awhile while the doctor pondered. "Could I talk to Molly alone for a minute?" she asked Mom, who looked a bit taken back by the request, but nodded her head nonetheless. What was she going to say? No? "You can wait in the waiting room," the doctor offered. "I'll come get you in a minute." Mom left with a confused look, and this gal turned to me. "Molly, I think I know how you got these. You did this to yourself, didn't you?"

I rode this out as long as I could. "What do you mean?"

She gave me a look that said, nicely, don't take me for stupid. "What I mean is that from the location of these cuts and the fact that they're on your left arm, I don't think anyone or anything else did it to you. There's also no way this could happen without you being aware of it." She let that reality sink in me for awhile, waiting for me to respond. I didn't. "So?" I looked out the window. It was more rain now than snow. Pretty gloomy.

"Molly!"

"What?" I was getting irritated. I didn't like being cornered.

"Molly, please, look at me." I turned a bit. "I think you did this to yourself. I don't know why, but there must be something really bothering you. I need to know, Molly. Have you had any thoughts of hurting yourself?" I looked at her like, what a dope!

"Let me be more specific. Have you thought about killing yourself?"

You know, that was the million dollar question. Did I feel like killing myself? A more accurate question might be, did I felt like living any more? Absolutely not! Did I feel like killing myself? If that meant I wouldn't have to see the world through my own putrid, goddamn, despicable eyes, then I guess the answer would be yes. "No, I haven't," I answered, staring her right in the eyes.

"Molly, listen. By law, I'm required to make a report any time I have reason to believe someone might hurt or kill themselves."

I was ready for this game of Chicken. "I just told you, I'm not thinking of it. I have absolutely no intention to kill myself."

She shifted back and forth, trying to decide what to do next. "Molly, I'll tell what we're going to do." (Again with the "we" stuff!) "I'm going to give your mom the name of some psychologists who work with teens, and I'm going to tell her to make an appointment for you. I expect you to keep it. It's either that, or I make a call right now to the Crises Center that deals with these kinds of situations, and you and your mom get in the car and go there right now. What's it going to be?" This girl could play Chicken, too.

"Whatever."

"So you'll do it?"

"Do I have a choice?"

"No."

"Then, like I said, whatever."

"Also, Molly, would it be OK if I explained this to your mom?"

"That depends. What are you going to tell her?"

"You can be here when I tell her, but what I'll tell her is that I think you're in a lot of distress over something, and that the cuts were self-inflicted. I'll tell her that I want you to see a therapist, and that I want to know when the appointment is scheduled. I'll tell her that I don't want you alone until you have that appointment, and until your therapist said you're OK. Any questions?"

"No." What was I going to say? She had me cold. Part of me also knew I needed to talk to somebody, so what the hell did I have to lose?

She called my mom back in, and described the situation to her pretty much the way she said she would. I watched my mother's face as the doctor talked. She looked like she was trying to stay cool, but I noticed the blood draining a bit from her face when she heard about the cutting. Mom nodded her head at the appropriate times, asked some appropriate questions, took the paper the doctor gave her with the shrinks' names on it, and thanked her. The doctor put some antiseptic stuff on my cuts, and gave me and my mom some instructions on how to keep the cuts clean and healing. My mom shook her hand and we left, with mom stopping at the reception area to do whatever it is parents do with the bill, insurance, etc.

We walked without words to the car, got in, and pulled out of the parking lot, heading home. Mom didn't talk the whole way home, and that was fine with me. The weather certainly matched the mood. It was dark, gray, and cold. Actually, I was expecting the third degree and was somewhat relieved when I didn't get it. We walked into the house, and Mom left me in the living room. Did you ever have one of those times when parents were so upset that they actually said nothing, did nothing, yet it was dramatically more intimidating than if they scream to the max? This was one of those times. Funny, though, I couldn't have cared less. Maybe now, my mother had a clue. Maybe now, she was feeling a bit of the desperation I'd been living with for a long time. Maybe now. Or, maybe not. One of the changes I didn't like was the way she was looking at me now, like I was damaged goods, or crazy or something. Also, she looked mad! Pissed off! Like I had done something to her. She was slamming things around, moving fast and jerky, and otherwise sending ticked-off signals. I couldn't have cared less. If she was waiting for me to respond somehow, she'd be waiting for a long time. I heard her make some phone calls, and I figured she was trying to schedule an appointment for me. After a few muffled calls, she came into the living room, announced "You have an appointment on Tuesday after school. Don't make any plans until then," and walked out in a huff. Fine.

My brother came home from his job, completely unaware of what had gone on. "Hey," he said to me.

"Hey," I answered back.

He walked into the kitchen and said "Hello" to my mother. She basically grunted in his direction, and kept on chucking all available small objects to produce maximum noise. He walked back into the living room and asked, "What's the matter with her?"

"It's a long story," I answered truthfully.

He looked confused. "Why? What happened?" Poor guy.

"Don't ask."

"She's not mad at me, is she?" He looked worried.

For the first time in a long time, I laughed, much to my own surprise, albeit somewhat sardonically. "No, It's not you. It's me."

His look of relief was shortly followed by a look of puzzlement. "Why?" he asked. "What did you do?"

"It's a long story," I repeated. "Believe me. You don't want to know."

"Actually, you're right," he said glibly. "I don't want to know. I just don't want to step in whatever shit you've left laying around." Sensitive guy. Who said siblings don't bond anymore?

"Don't worry about it."

"Don't worry, I won't," he said, and bounced up to his room. He didn't need much persuasion.

A short time later, Mom stuck her head out, yelled "Dinner," and we gathered in the kitchen. Mom and I sat there under tension that was as thick as a morning fog in the fall, while poor Josh was just wolfing down the food as usual, oblivious to the storm. He tried to make some small talk, which went absolutely no where. Mom was stabbing the meat like it needed killing again, and I was not eating a damn thing. After a little while, Josh innocently piped up. "What's going on here? Why is everybody so miserable?"

Mom threw her fork down on the plate, glared at me, and spit, "Why don't you ask your sister?" Her lower lip was quivering, and the tears were tipping over the edges of her eyes. She pushed her chair back hard, jumped up and left the room, went into her bedroom and slammed the door.

Josh looked stunned and confused. "What the <u>hell</u> was that all about? What did you do?"

I was sitting there, wondering what to tell him, not wanting to tell him anything at all. I was sitting there, feeling the breathing getting choppy, and the vision getting cloudy, and the heart beating wildly. I was sitting there, with the my feet and hands starting to twitch, and my leg bouncing up and down. I was sitting there, torking up. I was sitting there, and the urge to cut was overwhelming. I was hyperventilating again, and I got up and stumbled to my room. God damn it, I <u>hate</u> this! I hate this! And, almost without realizing I was doing it, I found myself with the razor in my hand, my shirt up, and I was cutting my stomach, again, and again, and again. Back and forth, up and down, and back and forth.

All of a sudden, my mother was standing there, and she was screaming. Not anything in particular, just screaming. She reached down and grabbed my wrists with a strength I never knew she had. Josh appeared behind her, and he was standing there with this dumb look on his face, like he just made a left turn into hell. Mom twisted my wrist hard, and I dropped the razor on the floor. She scooped it up with her spare hand.

"What is <u>wrong</u> with you?" Mom screamed in my face. "What is <u>wrong</u> with you?" and she was yelling hysterically.

I stared her right in the eye, calm as can be. "It's my razor, Mom. I want it. <u>Give</u> me the goddamn razor. <u>Give</u> <u>it</u> <u>to</u> <u>me!</u>" I was screeching at her, and she was crying and wrestling with me, and Josh was standing there.

"What's the matter with you, Molly? What's the <u>matter</u> with you?" she asked, half-wailing, half-crying.

I didn't answer. What was the point? We stayed frozen in this emotional trance for what seemed like forever, with Mom looking at me like I was from the Village of the Damned, and me feeling 100% empty. Nothing there. Not a damn thing. Nothing good. Nothing bad. Just nothing. We were like some macabre performance-art scene. After awhile, Mom was sobbing, I was bizarrely calm, and Josh was paralyzed. Slowly, Mom eased her grip on my wrists and let go. She let the razor drop on the floor. We stood there, looking at each other, the emotion leaking out of us. For the first time in my life, I looked at her and saw an aging woman. Wearily, without comment, she turned and left the room, picking up the razor on her way out. Josh gave me a glance that said "Psycho-sister," shook his head, and walked out.

I looked down and realized my shirt was still pulled up. I reflected on my cuts, and studied their shape; how the razor made a red line that looked straight at first glance, but was actually a bit jagged and rough if you looked at it closely; how the skin folded back just a little bit where it was parted along the cut; how it was hard to judge the true depth of the cut, which looked thicker in the middle and thinner at the edges where the razor engaged the skin and then left it; how the color was actually quite varied, with bright red along the top edge of the cut, a bit of white along the lower edge of the slice, and a darker red in the crease of the cut; how the cuts looked like they were all random at first, but seemed to merge into a purposeful pattern if you studied them long enough, like abstract art. They were actually quite beautiful.

I was quite tired now, and dropped on my bed. My ceiling was waiting for me, and I shared the events of the day. The ceiling understood. It always listened, never asking embarrassing questions. At some point I fell asleep, I think. (I have a hard time telling the difference between conscious and unconscious anymore.) I'm guessing it was sleep because I was doing something similar to dreaming. In this dream, or whatever, I was somewhere with my father. Have you had dreams where you're somewhere you've never been before but, somehow, the setting seems familiar? Well, that's where we were. It was similar to a living room with big, overstuffed chairs and a roaring fire in a fireplace. Weird! We don't even have a fireplace. There were pictures on the wall and a coffee table that looked like the one at Mom's house. In the dream, I was wondering why it was there. We were sitting in these chairs like we'd always been there, and Dad was asking me how I was doing, how I was feeling. I was trying to explain, but the words that were coming out of my mouth weren't the ones I was thinking, and I was feeling panicky and confused. My father kept looking at me with a confused look, and kept asking me questions about the nonsense that was coming out of my mouth. With each question he asked, I struggled even more to tell him what I was thinking, what I was really feeling, but the responses were even more ridiculous and disconnected. He was getting irritated with me, insisting that I "start making sense" or he was going to leave me. When he threatened this, I got really scared in the dream, and tried super-hard to say what was in my head, to do what he wanted. This time, though, nothing came out; my mouth just moved and no sound came out. He was furious and yelled, "I don't have a daughter anymore!" With that, he turned, slammed the door, and walked out. I jumped up and ran to the door, yanked it wide, and tumbled into a dark, open space. I plummeted with the sensation of falling faster and faster and faster, trying to scream but with nothing coming out.

I woke up with that jolt you get in these kinds of dreams when you subconsciously hit bottom. I hurt my neck I jerked so hard. My eyes sprang open and I laid there, disoriented, breathing fast. I looked around the room and the objects in it were spooky silhouettes. The only sound was my breathing, although I swore I could hear my heart beat. I rolled over and glanced at the clock on my dresser, which looked like a lighthouse with the glowing LEDs, and the time was 2:06 a.m. I would have sworn it was much later, near morning, and I was deeply disappointed it wasn't. I rubbed my hand over my bedspread, and the motion made a soft sound similar to waves of heavy rain rolling down a window in a sudden summer storm, and I kept doing it, finding some reassurance in the fact that I could control it.

I figured it was gonna be another long night. For reasons I don't comprehend, I started humming. At first I wasn't sure what I was humming, although it sounded familiar. After humming for awhile, I suddenly recognized the tune; it's a hymn we used to sing when I was a little child in children's services at church. Talk about peculiar. Now that I remembered it, I started to softly sing the words: "Yes, Jesus loves me/ Yes, Jesus loves me/ Yes, Jesus loves me/ The Bible tells me so." I sang it over, and over, and over, and I found it comforting and soothing, reassuring and relaxing, although I wouldn't read too much into that, like now I had religion or something. All I knew was it was helping, and that was good enough.

Yes, Jesus loves me.
Yes, Jesus loves me.
Yes, Jesus loves me.

The Bible tells me so.

CHAPTER 6

The next couple of days went by like most did: fuzzy, repetitive, boring, and long. Sun came up, sun went down. First bell rang, last bell rang. The home was tense but polite, as we were all acutely aware of the smoldering embers that could re-ignite with the slightest emotional breeze. Despite knowing somewhere in the back of my mind that this appointment was looming, I really didn't dwell on it much. Kind of a big "Oh, well."

Mom picked me up from school, waiting in the lobby for me to come out. I guess she wanted to make sure there were no last minute escapes out the window or something. We drove to this office building in town that I recognized but had never been in, and Mom parked the car. We went in and she tracked down the location on the office directory in the hall - "Robert Raimes, Ph.D., Clinical Psychologist." A fun elevator ride to the appropriate floor, a stroll down a hall, and an entry into a waiting room with the predictable receptionist, chairs, and how about this, assorted piles of "People" magazine! Gosh, it's good to know there's some things you can count on! Mom announced our presence and we sat and flipped through the magazine pages, like all good sheep, until this guy appeared. "Hi," he said in a collective sort of way to the both of us, and then turned toward me asking, "Are you Molly?"

"Yes, this is Molly," Mom answered, despite the fact she hadn't been asked.

"I'm Dr. Raimes," he said and reached out his hand. I extended mine, and we shook. He turned to my mother and shook her hand, too, with the usual introductory banter. "C'mon in," he said to me, and I got up and started to follow him into this office. "I'm going to talk to Molly for awhile," he informed my Mom, who nodded and sat back down to further explore the glossy worlds of the Rich and Pointless.

The "inner sanctum" was not pretentious. A couple of easy chairs, a couch (there had to be a couch!), a coffee table, bookcases, lamps, etc. Pictures on the wall, plants on the stand, and curtains on the windows. "Have a seat," he said, motioning to the easy chairs as he sat in one. I paused, considering my options. "Don't worry," he suggested with a grin, "Your seating choice is of no significance," and I smiled and plopped in the nearest one. "Molly, I want to get to know you, so I'm going to ask you some things about stuff like school, what you like to do, your family and friends, and so on. What you say to me will stay between you and me unless you tell me it's OK to discuss it with someone, and then I'll give you an idea of what I'll be discussing. The only exception is if I believe you're going to do something to hurt yourself or somebody else. I have to tell somebody if I think that. OK?"

"Actually, I've already heard something like that."

"Oh, really? Where?"

"From the school counselor and the doctor who sent me here."

"So, you've been around," he said with a smile.

"More than I want to be," I answered honestly. He proceeded to ask me things about various aspects of my life, none of which were too threatening, and I thought to myself, so far, so good. Ain't too bad. He asked me about my home and who lives in it. I chuckled.

"Why are you laughing?" he asked.

"Which home are you referring to?"

"So, are your parents separated or divorced?"

"Divorced."

"How long?"

"Since I was little." We proceed to talk about the whats, the whens, and the whys as far as I could see them. We talked about the schedules, the comings and goings, and the days and nights spent here and there. We talked about the holidays and the summer vacations, and times I wanted to be with Dad when with Mom, and with Mom when with Dad. We talked about the Christmases that were "democratically" split between two homes with two trees, two holiday dinners, two present-opening ceremonies, one Santa strangely coming down the chimney at two different houses for the same two kids, two parents who were jealous when we were with the other, and two kids who always felt personally responsible for their hurt feelings.

"Sounds like it's been a bit confusing," he suggested.

"You don't know the half of it."

"How about school? What grade are you in and where do you go?" We then embarked on a journey into my academic career to date, and I shared some of my reflections on the acquisition of the three Rs. I laughed again inadvertently when he inquired about what subjects I liked the best, and he asked, "What's so funny?"

"Oh, I don't know," I answered, "the terms liking and school don't seem to belong together in the same sentence."

"Well, you must find some subjects more tolerable than others."

"Actually, I used to like English and Art, but I have a hard time paying attention anymore."

"How long has that been the case?"

"I'm not quite sure, but at least as long as I've been in high school."

"So, would you say that high school has been a disappointment so far?"

"No, I think I've been a disappointment so far."

"Why would you say that?"

"I thought that's what you're supposed to tell me."

He smiled and said, "I can probably help you figure that out, Molly, but I don't have a crystal ball that gives magic answers. If I did, I'd be rich."

"Shit!" I blurted out, and then realized I was cursing (again). "Oops, sorry."

"What are you sorry for?"

"For the language."

"Look, Molly, I don't like cursing myself, but it's a pretty normal response to stress."

"So you don't mind?"

"This isn't about me, Molly, it's about you. Don't worry about it. I'm not wild about it but if I think it's a bit much, I'll just let you know. So, again, why do you think you're a disappointment?"

"Because."

"Because why?"

"I don't know why."

"You just do," he suggested.

"Yeah, I do."

"Molly, one of the things we'll do is try to figure that out. It can get to a point where nothing seems to make a whole lot of sense, and you can feel like a failure in most everything and not have any real specific reasons why. Have you ever talked with anybody else about this?"

"Not much, a few times."

"With who?"

"A counselor in school tried. My mom's tried a couple of times."

"No good?" he asked.

"No. Most people just try to tell you why you're wrong, and why you should feel so fortunate and blessed. You know, the 'starving children in the world and how you're lucky to not be one of them' speech. I hate that kind of shit. Ah, oops, sorry. I did it again."

He chuckled. "How do most of those discussions make you feel?" he asked.

"Guilty," I responded.

"So you felt guilty most of the time, don't you?"

"No, <u>all</u> the time. How'd you know?"

"Molly, it may come as a surprise to you, but you're not alone. There's a lot of kids who feel just like you do. There's a whole lot of pressure out there to do good. You know, to get the best grades, to be the best athlete, to be the prettiest, or the wittiest, or something."

"Well, so far, I'm not doing so good."

"Why do you say that?"

"Because I screw up most everything I touch."

"Like what?"

I thought for a minute, deciding which disaster to divulge. "Like my grades, for example. They're pitiful."

He looked back at his notes, obviously looking for something, and then stopped like he found it. "I thought you told me your grades were about in the 80s."

"I did."

"Well, then, help me here. That's about a B average, isn't it?"

"Yeah, so?"

"So, what's horrible about that?"

"I should do a lot better. Everybody else does."

He smiled and said, "And I should have thicker hair, too. Everybody else does. I don't know many of us who are doing our best in all the stuff in our lives all the time. Do you think it's realistic to expect that much of yourself?"

"Yeah, well, I'm not doing it anywhere."

He paused for a second or two, and then said "So, you feel like you don't meet anybody's expectations of you, anywhere in your life, do you?"

"I not only feel it. It's true."

"According to you," he pointed out. I flashed a dirty look in his direction. "You look like you didn't care for that last statement," he said.

"Sorry, but it's kind of like your calling me a liar, like I'm making it up."

"I'm sorry, too, Molly, that's not my intention. However, what we're talking about are your feelings, not some kind of fact like an answer on a math test. What you call a failure somebody else might call a success. What you see as a fault somebody else may see as a quality. Depression can make everything in life seem lousy, no matter what the truth is. It's like looking at life through glasses that are smeared with Vaseline. Nothing seems clear, nothing makes any sense. And, if by chance something starts to look good, depression smacks you in the side of the head and says, 'Hey, don't be stupid, don't believe it, it's lying to you.' It's like the devil whispering inside your ear, telling you to put yourself down. To blame yourself for everything. To doubt yourself. Depression can be a liar, a big-time liar."

"So, what are you saying, my problem is depression?"

"At least partly. Yes, I believe it is," he answered.

"And my life's just fine?" I asked, with more than a bit of skepticism in my voice.

"No, I'm saying your life has a lot of aspects to it, some of which are probably stressful and hurtful right now, and some that aren't as bad as depression would like you believe, or won't let you see as problems you might be able to do something about. The trick is to be able to look at those problems as situations that had a beginning, and as situations that can have an end. The problem isn't you, Molly, it's depression."

"So, what does that mean? I'm supposed to just whistle a happy tune and move on?"

He laughed a bit an said, "I wish it were that simple. But, the first step is to know that you have more power and control than you think you do, at least in regard to how you decide to look at the problems in your life. That can change." He paused for a moment. "Let me give you an example. Can you recall a time when you were a little kid and were scared of the dark, or something like that?"

"Sometimes."

"Can you give me an example?"

I stopped and thought. "Well, I remember when I was about five hearing some funny noises outside my bedroom that got me screaming, and both my parents came running into my room. They said I sounded like I was being murdered or something"

"And what did they turn out to be?"

"It was the wind, or at least that's what my parents told me."

"And were they right?"

I smiled. "Well, it wasn't the bogeyman, if that's what you mean."

"So, you did survive the night?" All of this was said with a mildly ironic tone.

"I guess so," I admitted. "Sorry."

He looked at me for a minute. "Do you realize how many times you've said 'sorry' since you've been here?"

"Oh, sorry!" I answered almost automatically, and then grinned sheepishly when I realized I did it again. He laughed. We talked some more about topics like my school and how I felt about the other kids and my teachers. We talked about what I like to do, or at least what I used to like, and when I stopped liking. We talked about my feelings, and he asked me to describe what makes me happy, mad, sad, and so on. As I was talking about being sad, I started to cry, even though I swore to myself earlier that I wouldn't, and he handed me a box of tissues. I resisted the urge to apologize again, and struggled to gain control. Impulsively, in my frustration I smacked the arm of the chair I was sitting on.

"Do you do stuff like that a lot?" he asked.

"Like what?"

"Like hitting things when you're upset?"

"No," I answered, more honestly than not.

"Do you do other things when you're frustrated or upset?"

"Such as?" I asked, confused.

84

"Like hurt yourself?" He was looking right in my eyes. I didn't answer and turned away.

"So, how do you do it?"

"Do what?" I responded, not sure what he meant.

"Hurt yourself." He was fairly calm, fairly matter-of-fact about it.

Trying to dodge, I answered with "I didn't say I did."

"You also didn't say you don't."

Silence.

"Do you cut?"

Shit! Found out again!

"You do, don't you? On your arms?"

I nodded.

"Anywhere else?"

Silence.

"On your stomach?"

I nodded.

"On your legs?"

I avoided his glance.

"Pretty much anywhere you think you can without being found out, right? Do you hit yourself, too, or do other stuff?"

"Not as frequently," I answered.

"But you do sometimes."

"Sometimes."

"Molly, most of the other kids I've worked with who cut are surprised to find out that they're not the only ones who do it, but believe me, you're not alone. There are a lot of kids who cut, and most of them are not only embarrassed they do it, they're ashamed of themselves, and feel like they're real freaks for doing it. They're terrified others will find out, and go to amazing lengths to hide the fact that they do it. But it's a habit that once it starts, it can be real hard to break, and you can end up feeling like some kind of 'pain junkie' who needs a fix. The more you do it, the more ashamed of yourself you get. The more ashamed you are, the more you feel the need to cut."

I was sitting there listening to this guy, and it was as if he peeked into my brain. I almost felt embarrassed, like realizing you've been walking around with a big piece of food sticking out of your teeth all day. We talked some more about me, which was a bit easier to do after the cutting stuff was out of the closet, because it was sort of the worst thing he could have uncovered. Now that he knew it, I felt like there wasn't much to risk, so I think I relaxed a bit.

"So," he said, "we're starting to run a bit low on time here." I was surprised. It only seemed like I'd been there for a month or two! "What I'd like to do is see you here about once a week for awhile to work on some of this stuff. I know it's not always fun, and I'm sorry some of this got you upset, but it's generally true that once you're able to talk about the stuff, it's a bit less threatening, and it usually gets easier to see ways you can deal with it. Are you game?"

I thought about it for a moment or two. "OK," I said. I figured, what have I got to lose? The way things were going, I needed something. I also figured it couldn't hurt politically, and maybe my mother wouldn't be climbing down my throat about the cutting. I also figured I wasn't going to have a whole lot of choice about it. He didn't seem like a bad guy, and this meeting went better than I thought it would.

He reached over to one of those card holder thingies on an end table, took out what I assume was a business card, and wrote something on the back of the card. "Here," he said, "this is my card and it has my office number on it. I also wrote my home phone number and pager number on the back." He paused and looked right at me. "Molly, I want you to hear this." He paused again for what I'm assuming was dramatic effect. "If you ever feel really stressed, or really depressed or sad, or really angry or mad, or really anything that's upsetting to you, I want you to know that you can call me at any of these numbers, any time. Do you understand?"

I nodded.

"Also, Molly…" (There was more?) "I'd like you to look at me and tell me that you'll call me, or talk to your parents, or a teacher, or somebody if you ever get the urge to hurt yourself. That can be like an urge to cut or to hurt yourself some other way, or an urge to kill yourself. Do you ever get thoughts about killing yourself, Molly?" he asked, staring right in my eyes.

"Sometimes, yes," I told him, looking to the side to avoid his gaze.

"Have you ever tried to kill yourself?"

"Not really."

"What does that mean?"

I looked up at the ceiling, trying to figure out how to respond to this. "What it means is that I've wondered about how I could do it. Like, sometimes, when I'm cutting, I think how easy it would be to just pull the blade across my wrists instead of the other spots I pick. I figure it would just be a bit more blood than I'm used to, not that big a deal. I've also thought about sitting in the car in the garage and starting it because I remember reading somewhere about somebody else famous doing that to kill herself."

"Any other times?"

"A couple of times." God, this wasn't easy.

"Such as?"

"A few times I've had an urge to drive our car over those steep cliffs on the road up on East Mountain. Once, the feeling was real strong and I wasn't even feeling bad at the time. It was like this feeling just came to me when I was there. I just thought how quick it would be, just done. I had to slow down and pull to the side of the road because I really felt I could do it. I got scared then because it seemed like such a good idea, like the big answer." I'm telling him this stuff like I'm talking about a day in the park, but I'm with it enough to recognize that it's really weird that I don't give a shit.

"Why didn't you?" he asked, looking at me intensely.

I shifted around a bit in the chair. "Why didn't I what?"

"Kill yourself."

I thought, and thought, and thought. "I don't know. Really, I don't. I think there was a small part of me that knew it was nuts to believe it was a good idea. I also worried about it not going well."

"What do you mean not going well? That you wouldn't die?"

"Yeah, that's right. I thought, I'm such a screw-up, with my luck, I'd only injure myself and end up living in some damn nursing home or something. Then I'd have to live with everybody coming to visit and feeling sorry for me, acting like they gave a damn and there I'd be, stuck on some kind of machine or something. Usually, by the time I was done thinking all this stuff, the feeling would pass."

"So, you're not feeling like dying these days?" he asked.

"No, actually, I feel like I'm already dead."

"How would you describe it?"

"Describe what?"

"Feeling dead."

"Oh. Well, actually, it's just basically feeling nothing."

"Nothing?"

"Yeah, nothing. Flat. Empty. Actually, it used to hurt more than it does now. Now, I'm just kind of numb. Nothing excites me much anymore. I just sorta go through the motions."

"Have your friends noticed?"

"A few. Some have asked me what's wrong but after a while I think they just believe you're being weird or dramatic or something. They just kinda let me be."

"And that's just fine with you, isn't it?"

I gave him a smile, one of the few I'd given him. "Yeah."

"Well, I'm not going to do that."

I was confused. "Do what?"

"Just let you be."

"What do you mean?"

"Just like you found out when you were little that the spooky things you were convinced were outside your door weren't real, you also can find out that the spooky things inside your head aren't real, either."

I was a bit offended by his casual disregard for my perceptions. "So, I'm crazy, or something? Is that what you're saying?"

"No, no, not at all. What I am saying is that these problems, bad as they are, can be fixed, or will pass, or can go away. I'm saying that you have more control than you think you do. I'm saying that you've got choices, but the choice of killing yourself, or being dead, aren't choices. They're just the end, the end to everything. Imagine...," he said with a wistful voice, "imagine that you, unlike me, actually have a crystal ball."

"OK," I said, thinking this guy was going off the deep end here.

"All right, now imagine that you look into that ball, and can see 10 years, 15 years, 20 years into the future. In this future, you see yourself. And, lo and behold, you're not only OK, you're happy. Really happy. You feel content, comfortable, safe."

"Yeah, right," I responded skeptically. "Fat chance."

"How do you know it couldn't happen? Can you tell the future?"

"No, but I can guess."

"Than why not guess happy?"

I paused. "I don't know."

"I think I have a reason. Depression won't let you, doesn't want you to. If you did, then you would see that it's possible that happiness is right around the corner, or down the road a year from now, or two, or three, or somewhere. If that's possibly true, than wouldn't it be worth sticking around to live it?"

"Hard to say, actually."

"Well, that's the job right now, Molly, to be able to say. To think about the possibility that you can and will be happy, to admit that it's possible. Your problems now, as overwhelming as they seem, and I'm not trying to minimize what you're going through as I'm sure they're as painful as you see them, these problems can have an end, and the beginning of that end is to start to believe that."

"That's a heck of a lot easier said than done," I answered.

"Yes, but still doable. It's about the possibilities, Molly. Life offers possibilities. Death offers nothing. Nothing good, nothing bad, just nothing. I don't know, maybe you're right, and your life will be the pits for ever, but I need to believe, you need to believe, we <u>all</u> need to believe that there are possibilities, or otherwise we're all lost. Let me ask you this, Molly. Imagine, again, (you'll notice that I use that word a lot), imagine that you're walking down a street and notice a little kid run into the street, and she's not paying any attention at all. You also notice that there's a car coming down the street, and rush out and pull this child onto the sidewalk, just before she would have been hit by that car. You probably saved this kid's life, or at least prevented her from being hurt real bad."

"OK, cool, but so what?"

He paused for a long time before answering, and then said slowly, seriously. "Now imagine the same scene but this time, you're not there to yank this child to safety. You're dead. You killed yourself. This child, who might have lived if you did, now doesn't. What might have been, hasn't been."

This was spooky, kind of scary. "Wow, I never thought of it that way."

"Most of us don't, Molly. But I would argue that you don't know yet what purpose your life is to serve, but it certainly can serve a purpose. It may not be saving a life, but it may be something like making somebody happier because you're here. It may be raising children, or finding a cure for some disease, or being a friend to somebody when they really needed it, or <u>something</u>. Something, Molly. <u>Not</u> nothing. You just have to be around to see it happen."

Interesting angle. Certainly, not a way I'd looked at it before. I didn't respond. I just sat there quietly. I felt more confused than when I came in but, in a way, that's good. I didn't know why, it just was.

He broke the silence first. "Our time's up, Molly, I have another kid to see now. I know this is probably confusing right now, and that's OK. Sometimes, confusion is the beginning of learning. I hope I can help you learn something about yourself, because I suspect there are great things in you that just need the time and space to come out. Are you willing to work with me for awhile on this stuff?"

"Sure," I answered. "What the heck."

"And you'll remember what I said about calling me if you need to?"

"Yes."

"OK, great." He stood up. "It was good meeting you," and he reached out and shook my hand again.

"You, too," I said, and he led me out into the waiting room. He spoke briefly to my mother while I stood there, saying that he'd like to see me again next week, and at least weekly for awhile. Mom nodded, etc., and we all exchanged good-byes. Dr. Raimes invited his next patient, a nervous looking little boy, into his office and we went to the secretary, did the scheduling bit, and then left.

In the car on the way home, Mom asked how it went, how I liked it, and so on. I gave some muffled answers, "yes," "no," "I don't know," and other evasive responses. I admitted to her that I was OK about going back, because I felt like I needed somebody on my side. Somebody I could talk to who wasn't going to judge me, or be hurt by what I said or thought, who was not up to his damn neck in the family drama. I figured I'd give it a shot. It was already a bit less intense with Mom, and I was guessing she felt like she didn't have to carry the load all by herself. She seemed relieved, and she agreed she wouldn't give me the third-degree about what was discussed.

When we got home, I went up to my room and assumed the position. In a strange way, I felt more confused now than I did when I left, but it felt better, at least a little bit. It was kind of like having an advocate on my side, or at least somebody who didn't have a hidden agenda. I looked at the card he gave me, and figured I might as well hang on to it. I took my purse and stuck the card in it. Who knows? Maybe it would come in handy. I tried to take his advice to imagine the future, a future where my life didn't stink. The view was a bit fuzzy, and I sort of got a headache from trying. Oh, well, it was the first time. Maybe it gets easier with practice. I hope so. I kind of liked the thought of living in a world where I didn't hate myself. This needed some work.

CHAPTER 7

Another school week began, and I worked hard at maintaining my "Molly's not so bad off" posture. After all, the system wasn't asking for a whole lot in terms of appearances, and I could walk the walk and talk the talk if it kept the administrative wolves at bay. My mental health motivation waned a bit as time passed from my therapy session but, after all, nothing lasts forever. I didn't expect to walk out "cured" and I wasn't, but we'll see. A few days into the week at home in the evening, Mom yelled up to me that I had a call, announcing, "It's that boy, Craig." I was both surprised and not surprised, relieved and nervous, all at the same time (more conflicting feelings, but as they say, "been there, done that.") I ran down the hall, snatched the cordless from my mother's bedroom, and yelled to her that I had it. As I flopped on the bed in my room and clicked the phone on, I heard her hang up.

"Hello?" I said, tapping my endless supply of creative oratory.

"Hey," he responded enthusiastically, "How ya doing? I'm calling back as requested. What's up?" Damn! I had forgotten about blowing him off the last time he phoned. I was surprised he was calling back after the abrupt way I ended his last attempt.

"Nothing much. How about you?"

"The same, just school and all that stuff. Can you talk this time?"

"Hey, I'm really sorry about cutting you off like that last time. It was so rude."

"Don't worry about it," he said sincerely. "I'm sure you had a good reason. I didn't take it personally."

"I'm glad," I told him with a flood of relief. We chatted awhile about the basics, and I relaxed more and more the longer we talked. It was interesting how the same kind of mundane conversation you have lots of time with different kinds of people can have a different impact, ranging from a yawn to excitement, depending on who you're talking to. I went through this same kind of conversation many times each week with various people with only minor variations. You know, the small talk routine. Only this time, it felt interesting and exciting. What's up with that? We talked and talked, and I laughed and so did he, which was amazing to me because my sense of humor had taken a dive as of late. However, talking to him, I felt comfortable enough that my inhibitions disappeared for awhile, and the clouds in my head and heart parted a bit. I actually felt (dare I say it?) good! It was an emotion that was noticeable but hard for me to label because I've felt it so rarely as of late. Before I knew it, my mom yelled up, "Molly, it's getting late. How much longer are you going to be on the phone?" I looked over at the clock on my dresser and I was surprised to notice that an hour and a half had gone by. I guess it is true that time flies when you're having fun.

"Not much longer, Mom," I yelled back.

"OK," she responded calmly. I think she would have been hard pressed to give me grief about it. She was well aware of the self-imposed isolation I'd been living.

I broke the news. "Craig, I've gotta go. School night and all that."

"Yeah, I guess it is kinda late. Hey, what about this weekend? Do you want to do something? Go see a movie or something?"

"Sure, that sounds like fun." Fun? Wait a minute, what the heck is that? Fun? I may need to look it up in the dictionary.

"OK, then, I'll give you a call on Friday."

"Sounds good."

"All right. Good-bye."

"Good-bye," and we both hung up. I plopped the phone on the floor and laid there, reflecting on the fact that optimism lived again when I had certainly pronounced it DOA a long time ago. I was feeling things I couldn't recall feeling before, with the possible exception of the "crush" type of things you do when you're little that are as much play and make-believe as real. However, this was different. It seemed that, for the first time, there was somebody out there who had an interest in me as me, emotional warts and all. True, he didn't yet know what a basket-case I was, but I sensed that wouldn't matter. I couldn't recall a time when I was able to talk to the opposite boy-sex so calmly, so comfortably, and it was exciting in ways that were brand-spanking new to me. I was actually laying there and smiling! Damn! Imagine that! Smiling! I almost felt embarrassed even though there was nobody else there. This relationship stuff was strong medicine!

I called to my mom that I was going to bed, and did the usual nighttime routines before climbing into bed. As I turned off the light and laid there gazing up at my companion, the ceiling looked different for the first time in a long time. For the first time in forever, my focus was on the outside, and not inside my damn head. For the first time in ages, I was having a hard time sleeping, not because of the fog, but because of the light, which was blazing in my mind like a blinding sun on the first spectacular day of spring. I was laying there thinking that I could get used to this good weather. However, just as I thought that thought, I felt this sharp stab of panic that almost lifted me right off the bed. Alarmed, I tried to figure out why, and I realized in my fear that I was setting myself up for a big fall. I was used to despair. Suddenly, I was finding that hope was scaring the shit out of me, and the pessimism was pounding on my forehead to get in.

Well, the hell with you! Not tonight! I was going to feel good, so deal with it. I struggled to remember some of the things that Dr. Raimes told me, and I tried to fashion a vision of the future. OK, I had something coming through, a vision. In this vision, Craig and I were having a nice, uneventful relationship. We'd been an "item" for awhile and it seemed old and comfortable. He knew my quirks and flaws, and hadn't yet run screaming out the door! I was older, and we were both in college. Which college I couldn't tell you, but it had that "classic" college look, like you always see on TV where the dorms look like moss-covered Victorian mansions and the trees are always at the peek of fall color, with some red, yellow, and orange leaves falling gently to the ground while all these happy-looking students scurry excitedly to class. I was meeting Craig after class, and we were walking hand-in-hand to the Student Union, where we joined with a group of students and discussed interesting, meaningful things about life and what it meant. I was laughing and offering profound insights that everybody saw as deep but witty.

While I was wallowing in this fantasy, I felt the slimy tentacles of fear reaching out to me, trying to twist themselves around me to pull me under. Tonight, though, I was able to untangle them, unwrap them, and push them off to the side. They were still there, but I just wasn't paying as much attention to them as I usually did. Not tonight. They were sort of like having a barking dog next door, which could drive you nuts if you paid attention to it but eventually turns into background noise if you ignore it long enough. Tonight, I was in front, and I stayed that way. Tonight, I won! Sleep came, and it didn't feel like Death in training. It just felt like sleep. And that felt wonderful.

The next day, I woke up earlier than I usually did, and I actually got up out of bed without the usual pleading and prodding from my mother. It was Friday, and I was looking forward to the day, and it was all too weird. However, I was a few hours away from the weekend, which should hopefully lead to a Molly-Craig reunion. I was motivated. I got ready for school pretty quickly, actually ready to make it out the door early, and my mom was looking at me queerly like I was a character from the adolescent equivalent of "Invasion of the Body Snatchers." "What's with you today?" she asked with a curious expression.

"What?" I replied with a tone of what's your problem, even though I knew full well I was way out of character.

"You're perky today," she observed.

"No, I'm not," I lied. "I'm just getting ready for school. Isn't that what you're always hounding me about? I thought you'd be happy. Jeez, there's no pleasing you." Even then, though, when I was trying to give attitude, I knew I wasn't doing it with my usual morbid conviction.

"This wouldn't have anything to do with that phone call last night from you-know-who, would it?" she asked coyly.

I tried to register my phony indignation, but I was guessing that if the color of my face matched the sudden increase in skin temperature I was feeling, I was not real convincing. "What are you talking about?"

She was chuckling now. "Oh, c'mon, Molly, you're blushing!"

"I am not!" I protested uselessly.

"OK, whatever!" she said, modeling typical teen exaggeration, and we both laughed. God, this was the first fun exchange I could recall with Mom in a long time, and it felt good. "It's nice to see you laugh," she commented, and I smiled back in a way that let her know it was nice to be able to do it.

"You, too," I responded.

School became an exercise in endurance, but now it was because of my rush for the future, not my resentment of the present. Mr. Quinn called me down to his office in the morning on Friday to check up on me, as I guess I made his "endangered list." When he inquired about the status of my mood and feelings, he looked more than a bit surprised with either my positive response, my convincing tone when responding, or the combination of the two. "This sounds encouraging," he noted. "What happened to bring about this resurrection?"

"Oh, various stuff," I answered. I still didn't feel like pouring my heart out.

"Well, whatever it is, I'm glad to see you feeling more comfortable."

"Thanks."

"Can I check with you in a week or so?"

"If you want to."

"OK, let's do that. I'll just have you called down to the office around then."

"Fine. See you then," and I returned to class. For the rest of the week, I probably looked better in class although one just doesn't leap back into academic competency when you've mentally been off-line for as long as I was. However, I probably took better notes than I had in a long time. No, let me correct that. I took my first notes of <u>any</u> kind in any class for a long time. It helped pass the time and I figured I should mine this for all the positive press I could squeeze out of it.

At lunch, my compadres also observed the change. "Ain't you the life of the party these days," Rebecca commented. "What's gotten into you, and where can I get some of it?"

"Yeah, that's right," Jasmine confirmed. "You have been in a better mood the past couple of days."

"It's nothing," I said, hoping to call off the curious dogs. "Nothing."

"Ah, c'mon," Jennifer chimed in. "What happened? What's the story?" I could see all of them staring at me waiting for some kind of answer.

"It's <u>nothing</u>!" I insisted. "Stop bugging me about it. God, girls, get a life!" However, I was smiling when I was protesting, so I don't think anybody was buying it.

"OK, fine," Rebecca retorted. "Go ahead. Be like that. Don't let us in on your secret. See if we care," all said with good humor. "Speaking of the weekend" (which nobody was) "what's everybody doing?" Various responses sprang up, and some tentative plans were made among the members.

"How about you, Molly?" Jasmine asked. "What are you up to? Want to do something?"

"I don't know," I answered evasively. "I don't have any plans yet."

"Then do you want to do something?" she persisted.

I wasn't sure how to squeeze out of this noose. "I don't know if I can. I may have other plans."

Rebecca jumped all over this vague response. "Oh, and it's something that we can't join?" I didn't answer. I was a stone. The light flashed in Rebecca's brain. "You wouldn't be going on a <u>date</u>, would you, with that Craig dude? <u>Surely</u>, you wouldn't do that without telling all of us about it, would you? Your good buddies? Your best friends?"

Nabbed again! I <u>knew</u> I was blushing now, and Suzanne chimed in with "Wow, look at how <u>red</u> her face is!" which only made me even more crimson. Now they were all over me, and I knew there was no escape.

"OK, OK, I may go out with him, but it's <u>no</u> <u>big</u> <u>deal</u>. God, leave me alone, will ya?" But that only increased the catcalling and teasing. "You guys are a pain in the ass," I protested, but I couldn't stop smiling, which didn't help my pissed-off performance. They were relentlessly plugging for particulars when I was rescued by the afternoon bell and I scurried out gratefully.

The afternoon passed painfully slow but predictably, and finally the last bell sounded. Yes, the day actually ended, and I hurried home after hopping off the bus. I ran in and checked the answering machine, but there were no messages. OK, then, I turned on the tube and watched some soap operas to pass the time, and I thought to myself that the phrase "killing time" had to come to somebody while watching these shows. Talk about shallow and mindless!

However, today they were perfect, and I gazed at the screen with little recognition of what was going on and even less concern while Daphne cheated on Jeremiah. (Or is it the other way around?) Couldn't happen to a nicer couple.

Again, the wait provided me with another opportunity to ponder how bizarre time was, and how it could torture your mind like a nasty child tortures the family cat. Dangle the string of yarn, and then yank it away. Roll the ball and watch it slide under a table where the cat can't get it, no matter how hard it tries. See the cat bring home its prized kill and then pick the carcass up and chuck it into the woods while the cat watches in horror. Yes, time is a tease, and it rules. You don't mean a thing to it. The more you want of it, the less you get. The faster you want it to go, the more it crawls. I knew that sitting there and staring at the phone was inviting torment, but I couldn't help myself. I stared anyway. I do masochism real well, anyway.

Approximately two or three centuries later, the phone rang. I almost dropped the cordless phone on the floor as I reached for it, and I pushed the "On" button hard enough that I expected it to come out the other side. "Hello?"

I heard a somewhat-familiar voice say, "Can I talk to Molly, please?"

"This is Molly," I answered.

"Oh, hi! How ya doing? It's Craig." No shit! Stay cool, girl, stay cool.

"Hi, Craig. I'm good. How about you?"

"Great, Molly, great." Fascinating conversation so far. "I'm calling like I said I would. Are you still interested in doing something this weekend?"

"Sure, what have you got in mind?"

"Oh, I don't know. Maybe we could go to a movie, or we could go to the Tombs, downtown. It's an all-ages club now and there's a good ska band playing there Saturday night. Which sounds better to you?"

"I really don't care. They both sound good to me, but I don't think my mom would be too thrilled about the club idea. It's been a bit crazy here lately" (talk about understatements!) "and I don't think she'd be OK about that."

"Hey, that's cool with me, we can do the movies. Which one do you want to see?"

"I don't care. You pick."

"OK. There's that movie about that reincarnation stuff playing at the City Square. I'm a sci-fi nut and I love that kinda jazz, and it got great reviews. How's that sound? Is that all right? Do you like that stuff, too?"

"Actually, Craig, the idea of reincarnation sounds real good to me right about now. Maybe I could pick up some tips. That one would be fine."

"All right, then, we'll do that. Which show do you want to go to?"

"Hey, it doesn't matter to me."

"How about the 8:30 show? We could see that and then go get something to eat afterwards."

"That sounds good, Craig."

"OK, then. I'll come by and pick you up tomorrow at about 8:00. I think it might be crowded."

"That's fine. Are you prepared to meet my family?"

He laughed. "I think I can handle it. Are they prepared to meet me?"

"Hey, Craig, it's not you my mom's likely to worry about. It's me."

With a puzzled tone, he asked, "Why's that?"

"It's a long story, Craig. Maybe when you've got a day or two I'll explain it."

"OK, whatever." We talked a while longer about various topics, and it was relaxing and exciting all at the same time. We talked about the school week, the weather, and other real deep stuff but somehow, the small talk felt more important than it usually did. I was laughing at jokes

I'd usually scoff at, and he was asking me details and commenting about the things I was discussing that let me know he was really interested, which I found amazing in and of itself.

"Hey, Molly, I gotta go. My father needs the phone. So, I'll see you tomorrow?"

"OK. When do you think you'll be here?"

"I don't know. How about a quarter to eight? That'll give us enough time to get to the movies before it starts. I'll pick up the tickets tomorrow during the day just to make sure we can get in."

"That sounds good, Craig."

"All right, see you then. Bye."

"Bye." And we both hung up. I flopped down on the couch and marveled at the ability of such a simple conversation to elevate my spirits. I was reliving the conversation over and over in my head, and wondering what the next night would be like. I imagined the theater, the movie (which I honestly wasn't all that interested in before tonight!), and then the both of us sitting together at some casual restaurant, laughing, saying deep things, feeling really good. I knew there was no way to actually predict if reality would be anything like this but, gosh, it was fun to speculate on it, and that's all I really wanted to do. I was laying there smiling to myself, and hoping no one else caught me doing this because I must have looked ridiculous! However, I decided that happy ridiculous beat depressed ridiculous any day of the week. I was lounging here in ol' La-La Land again for awhile when I heard Mom's car pull in the driveway and I struggled to put on my usual "game-face" before she came in. Too much happiness is a suspicious to a parent as too much pain.

"Hi, Molly. How was your day?" Mom asked as she walked in the family room where I hanging.

"Fine, Mom. How was yours?"

"<u>Long!</u>" she answered with dramatic emphasis. She dropped her day-stuff on the floor and dropped into the nearest recliner. From the looks of Mom and the other adults I'd seen after a week at the job, I couldn't wait to be a grown-up and face the world of work. (Yeah, right!) She pried off her shoes and pulled the footrest to the recliner all the way out. She let out a sigh that sounded like it weighed 100 pounds, and briefly went catatonic. She closed her eyes in a way that resembled meditation more than sleep, and began breathing with a sound like one of those iron lung thingies I saw in an old movie once. IN and OUT. IN and OUT. IN and OUT.

"Hey, Mom, are you all right? Are you OK? Should I call somebody, or something?" I inquired with a teasing tone, knowing full-well that I was walking a fine line between good-natured kidding and getting killed if it was a particularly bad day, but what the heck! Walk on the wild side.

She opened one eye, squinted at me briefly and then slammed the lid shut again. "Go away," she said dryly, but with a small smile that let me know the water wasn't too hot. I figured I wouldn't push my luck, though, and I let her be for awhile, shuffling around the house to give her some space. However, the calm was broken for good when Josh came busting in the door from school. He hung out with various friends at various places after school, and seemed to try to time his return as close as possible to the actual serving of dinner. I suspect the ideal would be just as the steaming plate was hitting the table, but this time he had guessed badly as there wasn't any cooking going on.

"So, what's for dinner?" he asked with a hint of both impatience and concern. One thing about Josh - he tended to cut to the chase. Mom didn't respond, and he stood there stoically waiting for an answer, like Scooby-Doo waiting for a Scooby Snack, despite the fact that any fool should have been able to see that nothing would be forthcoming any time real soon. Not one to observe the obvious, he said, "Mom?" with a plaintive tone that was pitiful to hear.

"<u>What</u>?" she said with irritation, both eyes still welded shut, although I'd swear I could detect her glare through the eyelids.

"What's for dinner?" he said again, and I was figuring he deserved whatever disaster he got here. However, to my surprise, Mom didn't skewer him with her laser vision. Rather, she let out another super sigh, pushed in the end of the recliner, opened her eyes, and wearily got up.

"Hold on," she said, "let me see what we've got." She shuffled heavily to the refrigerator, opened the door, and surveyed the junkyard of leftovers inside. She reached in and grabbed some sauce that was hibernating there in a Tupperware container and plopped it on the counter. She then latched on to some kind of pasta in the cabinet, put some water in a pot on the stove to boil, and started to walk towards her bedroom to presumably change her clothes.

"So we're having pasta <u>again</u>?" Josh asked foolishly and with mild irritation. Mom just stopped dead in her tracks without turning around. She paused there for awhile, most likely trying to decide what implement to use to strangle him, but then just continued her trek without even turning around or responding. "What's <u>her</u> problem?" he asked me. I just shook my head and walked away.

During dinner, Mom tried to shake off the workday coma and make conversation about the upcoming weekend. Josh explained how he was going out with some friends to some kid's house to do a whole lot of nothing in particular. "How about you, Molly? Any plans?" Funny she should ask.

"Not tonight," I responded with full evasive maneuvers.

"Any for tomorrow?"

"Yes."

"What?"

"I'm going out."

"Where?"

"To the movies."

"With who?" You knew it would get to that, didn't you? Could you feel the buildup, the foreshadowing, the <u>tension</u>? The funny thing was that I didn't understand why I was so damn tense about it.

"With Craig."

<u>Then</u> I knew why I was tense. Mom put down her fork, looked at me with that "Holy shit! Molly's actually got a date!" look, and said "Really?" I've got to hand it to the woman, she didn't choke on her linguini while saying it.

"Yes, <u>really</u>!" I said with a don't-bug-me-about-it tone which I knew didn't have a chance of working. She was just sitting there, staring at me, like this is the most amazing news she'd heard since she won the Parent-Teacher Association raffle back when I was in fourth grade.

"<u>Really</u>?" she asked again with her voice now a notch higher. I slammed down my fork in irritation.

"<u>Yes</u>, mother, really. Why? Is that such a miracle? <u>God</u>!"

"No, no, that's not what I mean. I mean, I was just a bit suprised. You haven't told me much about him yet. I don't know much more than his first name" She was scrambling now, realizing that if she ticked me off enough she'd have a hard time getting any juicy particulars.

"What exactly do you need to know, Mom? What's there to tell?"

"Well, like where does he live? What grade is he in? How are you getting there? You know, that kind of stuff."

"He lives in town, he's a senior at Central, and he's picking me up. Anything else?"

Mom got this puzzled look on her face. "I thought before you said he was in your Math class at Marshall, which would make him a Junior." You know, that's the problem with spontaneous lies. They're so damn hard to keep in order.

Trying to regroup, I said, "Well, I <u>knew</u> you'd give me the third degree about it, so I told you what you wanted to hear."

She continued to look at me oddly. "And why would I want to hear that?"

I was dancing now! "I didn't think you'd like the fact that he was a Senior, and that he went to a different school."

"So your choice was to lie to me about it?" Her voice was going up, and I knew I was headed into choppy waters.

Summoning up all my sincerity, I looked at her and said, "I'm sorry, Mom. I shouldn't have done that, you're right. I should have told you the truth. But, the way things were going, I thought you'd be mad at me if I told you he was a Senior from another school. But, Mom, he's really a nice guy! He really is! There's nothing wrong with what we're doing. It's just a date, we're only going to the movies, and..."

Mom interrupted me. "Look, Molly, I'm not saying I necessarily have any problem with you seeing this boy. I certainly want to meet him, but I'd want to meet anybody you might go out with. Because it hasn't happened before, we've just never gone through this before, but I'm sure it can be OK. What I'm <u>not</u> happy with is being lied to, or deceived. Do you understand?"

I may be a dope, but I knew when to suck up when I really needed to. "Yes, Mom. I am sorry. It won't happen again. I am really sorry," all said with head down, eyes glancing away, and all the other trappings of capitulation.

"All right, then. As long as we understand each other. But I'm warning you, I wouldn't recommend lying to me again."

"OK, Mom. I won't." Life is a series of hurdles, some small, some large. I made it over that one. I took the victory and ran.

In the hall, Josh passed me and sneered in a low tone to avoid detection, "You're full of shit up to your ears! I would've been killed if I lied like that."

"Tell somebody who cares, bro," I hissed back. Another special sibling moment, and we both moved on with shared contempt. I went to my room and prepared for the evening. While I decked out in my usual skater look of baggy pants and sweatshirt, I spent a bit more time on the hair, the makeup, and other trappings. I was self-conscious while doing all this and actually felt a bit embarrassed, but what the hell! The time crawled, but eventually I heard the doorbell ring, right at 8:00. I ran down to the door and swung it open.

"Hi, again," Craig said as he stood there on the front porch. "Are you ready to go?"

"Yeah, just about. C'mon in!"

He walked into the foyer and, just as he did, Mom appeared in the hall. "Oh, hi!" she said with her voice going up, which is a typical Mom-thing to do when she's greeting others. "You must be Craig." Good guess! "I'm Molly's mom."

"Hi, Mrs. Mitchell. How are you?" he asked, reaching out his hand.

I winced as Mom extended her hand and said "I'm fine, Craig, and it's Ms. Wooding." Ouch! I never explained divorce protocol to him, or the damn name-game!

"Oh, sorry," he said, looking awkward, and he sort of shuffled in place.

Mom laughed and let him off the hook. "Don't think another thing about it, Craig. Don't worry about it. It's a common mistake. I get it everyday."

"Oh, thanks," he stammered, and any fool could tell his game plan for Mom introductory chatter was out the window. It was sort of like forgetting your first line in a school speech and then panicking and fading out completely.

"You're welcome, Craig. You're welcome," and Mom smiled with that adult look of isn't-it-cute-how-he screwed-up. "Please," she changed the subject, "come on in and sit down while Molly finishes getting ready." I was wondering what it was that I need to finish, but I played along. We walked into the living room and Mom gestured to the chairs in the room, and Craig sat nervously in one. "Molly, do you think Craig wants a soda or something while he's waiting?"

"I don't know, Mom." What was I, a mind reader?

"Well, why don't you <u>ask</u> him?" she said with the edge of exasperation, but still smiling.

OK, fine! "Hey, Craig, do you want a soda?"

He had the look of somebody caught in the middle. "No thanks," he answered.

"<u>No</u>, Mom, he doesn't want one." Parents!

"All right, then, but hurry up so Craig isn't waiting long." I was still wondering what it was I was supposed to be doing, but I figured I'd get my coat, check the hair one more time, etc., and then book outta there. When I came back into the living room, Mom was sitting on the couch along side Craig's chair, asking him about his school, his family, and other get-to-know-you-from-the-parental-perspective questions. Craig seemed to be doing OK, and nobody looked like they're gonna hurl, so I figured it was going well.

"Hey, Craig, I'm ready," I let him know, and he got up to walk with me to the door.

Mom called out before we got too far, "So, where will you kids be?"

"At the <u>movies</u>, Mom," I told her with a thinly veiled "duh" emphasis.

"Well, have a good time."

"Thanks, Ms. Wooding," Craig said with all political correctness, and we walked out the door to his car.

"Don't mind my Mom," I told him as we hopped down the porch. "She was dying with curiosity."

"She seems nice," he answered with sincerity.

"She's OK, as mothers go."

"Wait until you meet mine," Craig said.

"Why? What's up with her?"

"Oh, nothing. It's just that she can be really goofy around my friends, and she tries to look like she's really cool, and sometimes it just comes out funny. Actually, though, she is kinda cool, or at least my friends think so. She messes up trying to use the 'lingo' sometimes, but she knows she does and everybody just kind of laughs at her when she does it, but she doesn't seem to care. In fact, it's like she does it on purpose some times, but that's cool. That's just my mom."

"I look forward to meeting her."

He turned and looked at me as we were hopping in the car. "So, you're assuming there'll be another time?" he said slyly.

"Only if you play your cards right," I informed him as we both slammed the doors. Craig motored to the theater and we were talking back and forth on the way about this-and-that, and I felt more relaxed than I thought I would, especially since the meet-the-mother episode went well. We got to the theater and went in to the movies after Craig paid for the tickets, which was also an area of uncertainty as I didn't want to assume that he was going to pay for me. After all, I was a liberated woman or at least would like to think I was, and I didn't want him to think that I was expecting it. That's just another example of how damn complicated this stuff could be, and there were countless matters of protocol that needed to be worked out. I told him he didn't need to pay, and I did have money, but he said don't worry about it, it wasn't a big deal. So, for the moment, I figured I'd let it go at that. Besides, it was the first time in my life that somebody who wasn't in a Molly-Management position paid for me, and it felt kinda good, sort of flattering.

We proceed to watch this lame movie about various supernatural nonsense, but Craig seemed to enjoy it. We whispered comments back and forth during it, trying to be subtle because the place was fairly crowded, but occasionally he or I would chuckle or laugh a bit too loud, and there would be some borderline dirty looks from the patrons around us. Somehow, that just seemed even funnier, and we were struggling to keep it together. Eventually, the hero and heroine were reunited together in bliss for all eternity, and we left the theater and headed for a local diner that kids frequent a lot. We got a booth and ordered your basic burger and fries type of stuff, which neither of us ate much of because a.) we were talking too much and b.) you worry about looking stupid while chewing food! The check came and, chauvinist culture that we are, the waitress handed it to Craig, like of course the guy will pay for the food. I reached across the table and snatched the bill, and Craig piped up and said, "Molly, I can pay for this."

"I know you can, Craig, but you don't have to. I have money, too."

"Yeah, but really, the guy is supposed to pay for the stuff."

"Oh, is that so? According to who?"

"According to my father. He told me to make sure I paid for everything. He said if this was an actual date, the guy's responsible for paying."

"Oh, he did, did he? And what makes you think this is an actual date?" I asked in a teasing voice.

He mockingly squinted his eyes and said, "In contrast to what? An artificial date? Would we then use artificial money? And besides, are you dissing my dad, who I'll have you know is a widely acknowledged dating expert?"

"Well, Craig, you can tell him that this girl can pay for it, too. I can handle it. Besides, why is it fair that you should have to pay?"

Craig sat there pondering, and he did a highly exaggerated rubbing of the chin like he was <u>really</u> deeply thinking. He looked at me with mock seriousness and said, "Molly, you are <u>absolutely</u> right. YOU PAY!" and comically stuffed his money back in his pocket. We both cracked up as I counted out the bills to pay. We both agreed, however, to split the tip!

There was a hint of snow as we walked to the car, and it was cold and the clouds were hanging dark and low in the sky like they were ready to spill open from the weight of the water within. Craig turned the car fan to high as we pulled out of the parking lot, but it would be a while before our breath became invisible again. Either because we were so cold, or because we were talked out, or because he was driving me home and we both knew we were coming to the end of an evening that had been pretty neat and an evening we wished could go on, conversation was hard to come by for the first time. After a certain time, we both seemed aware of the silence, but we both sat there hoping the other would break it first. I stared out the window and felt uncomfortable for the first time that night, and it saddened me even though I knew it wasn't realistic to expect it to be endless spontaneity. Or maybe it was because sadness had been such a constant companion for me that I slipped back into it like I was an addict who couldn't kick the habit. You hated it, but God knows you were used to it. I wrestled with the feeling, and I was really pissed off because for a brief while, I thought I could kick it. I should have known better. But what was this all about? It had been a great night, and nothing had gone wrong. Why the hell was I overreacting to this? God, Molly, get a grip! What was wrong with me? Why was I such a loser? Suddenly, Craig's voice pierced my fog. "Hey, what are you thinking about?" he asked. "You got awfully quiet there all of a sudden."

"Nothing," I answered solemnly. "Just quiet." Suddenly, I wondered if this was going to be my life. Did

111

this thing own me? Was I powerless against it? Was it going to lurk around, spying on me, waiting until my guard was down and I saw some light, felt some hope, felt alive, and then slam the shades down on me? The thought scared the shit out of me, and I gasped.

Craig looked at me with this increasingly curious expression. "What's the matter? Are you OK?" He kept turning and looking at me while trying to keep his eyes on the road. What was I supposed to tell the poor guy? The truth? That he spent the night with a serious head case? If he had any brains, he'd run as fast as possible in the other direction. Let's face it, this was a fluke. While I was really starting to sink into this funk, Craig reached across the seat and took my hand. I flinched at first from the suprise of his touch, and it must have been confusing for him after the great night we had, and he pulled his hand back. "Sorry," he said, and he put both hands back on the wheel.

"No, Craig, it isn't you, really it isn't. It isn't," and I reached over and took his hand off the wheel. I gripped his hand tightly, too tight I guessed, as I could see his expression of sudden confusion from what he must have thought was a relatively simple thing. He didn't know then that there was no such thing as simple with me, and I started to think that it was hopeless. I was hopeless. Just as this thought came, Craig pulled in front of my house. Having been in the "zone" for awhile, I didn't even realize we were this close, and I felt disoriented for a second or two. He put the car in park but left it running. The radio played softly over the gentle rumble of the engine and the humming of the heater.

"Are you sure you're all right? You're not sick or anything, are you?" I smiled at the irony.

"Yes, Craig, I am sick. I really am. Sicker than you know. Sicker than you want to know." This was what I thought. What I said, though, was "No, Craig, I'm fine."

"Molly, I had a really good time," he said. "I really enjoyed it." He was looking at me, obviously waiting for my reply.

"I did, too, Craig. I did, too," even though I felt like I was just hanging on now. I felt like Cinderella who's carriage was going to turn into a pumpkin at any moment. Craig leaned over to my side of the seat and put his hands on my face. I could feel the combination of both warmth and coldness in his fingers and hands as they cradled the sides of my face, and he gently pulled my face a bit towards his as he puts his lips on mine. It felt really wonderful at first and I started to be in the moment, and then it happened. Instead of Craig's face, I saw the face of the unknown pervert who pushed his sloppy, drooling mouth on mine and stuck his disgusting tongue down my throat while I gagged. Instead of the nice after-shave I detected earlier as Craig sat beside me at the movies, I smelled the rancid breath of a guy who changed my life in all of about a minute or two of terror. Instead of the hands of a boy who had shown me nothing but gentleness, I felt the sweaty palms of a bastard who left my breasts black and blue as he ripped away my clothing, my dignity, and what was left of my self-respect. Instead of the excitement and eager anticipation I should have been able to feel, should have been entitled to feel, I felt dread, self-loathing, nausea, and disgust.

I lurched, almost leapt, back against the door on my side of the car, and Craig's hands briefly hung in the air as if frozen in place before he dropped them uncomfortably on his lap. His expression was one of shock, confusion, and borderline guilt, despite having done nothing wrong. Welcome to my world, Craig. Poor boy.

"I'm sorry, Molly. I'm really sorry." This was the second or third time he had apologized to me in one night after showing more consideration than I deserved. I tried to answer him, to tell him that this had nothing to do with him, to let him know that I was responsible, it was my fault, to warn him that I was out of my freaking mind, to spare him the misfortune of associating with a loony like me, to explain why I was lower than shit, to give him advance warning of what hanging with me could bring him. Instead, I started to cry, and as I did, the panic welled up inside and my worst nightmare started to materialize, complete with the tingling, the panting, and the shaking. I tried to control it, to stifle it, to prevent Craig from seeing me make the vampire transformation, and the harder I tried, the worse it got. I couldn't deal with this, I couldn't do this! I had to get away! I yanked on the door handle and stumbled out of the car.

"Molly! Where are you going?" Craig called out as I staggered up the driveway with the tears blurring my vision as I went, making the driveway look like it was smeared with Vaseline. "What's the matter?" His voice was farther away. I just kept going. There was nothing I could say. There was nothing I could do. I just had to get away. I ran into the side door of the house where I could hopefully avoid the rest of my family and into the kitchen.

"Is that you, Molly?" Mom called out from the family room.

"Uh-huh," I answered, half-croaking, but she must not have thought much of it as she didn't come out. I climbed the stairs to my room and looked out onto the street where Craig's car was still parked, and I could imagine him sitting there wondering what the hell happened, wondering what to do. But, of course, what was there to do? Nothing. Not a thing. Eventually, the car lights went on, and after a brief interlude, it pulled slowly away from the curb and down the street. I watched the taillights gradually disappear into the dark cold night, and I wondered if I'd ever see him again.

This was it. No more. No more. This was going to come to an end, right now. I sucked inside myself, kind of imploded, and looked around. It was dark and damp, sort of gross, and it smelled. The sounds were grating, and the edges sharp and stabbing. It was doom. It was hell. And I lived here. There was a strange sort of clarity that came with this realization, and I knew in an instant that this wasn't some kind of haunted house, or Shakespearean nightmare. This was me. This was my life. This is what I was. And I couldn't live with. I wouldn't.

I fell to the floor and took out the razor I had hidden from Mom, the one she didn't find. My razor lay in the fold of the mattress cover where I'd hidden it, and I took it out and then carefully spread the towel I'd taken from the bathroom out on the floor and sat on it with my legs folded. I looked at the razor, twisting it from side to side, and a little piece of metal suddenly looked like the ticket to freedom. I was not scared. I was not nervous. Actually, in some ways, I was more at peace than I had been for awhile, once I'd made the decision. If anything, I was tired, very tired. And I was sad. And I didn't want to be sad anymore. I thought about calling Dr. Raimes, like he said to, but I'd have been embarrassed to tell him how low I'd sunk. I couldn't endure disappointing one more person, even one who gave me an invitation to do so. One more thing, one last thing, to feel guilty about.

I held the razor between my thumb and index finger and turned it until the sharp edge was facing me. I twisted my other arm until my wrist was facing up, and I could see the thin blue line that threaded up and across my wrist from the right to the left like one of those little tributaries on a social studies map. A small thing. It wouldn't take much, but it could do so much. I lowered the razor to the left side of my wrist until I felt the sting of the blade, and I kept pressing until the blood started to flow. I slowly pulled the blade to the right across my wrist and when I sliced the blue line the blood started to pour out, deep, dark, and red, curling around the edge of my wrist and dripping onto the towel beneath me. I placed the razor on the towel before stretching out on my side and then laid on the carpet with my arm positioned on the towel, my head back and my eyes looking up at my trusty companion, the ceiling.

"*What are you doing?*" the ceiling asked, curious about my strange behaviors.

"Dying, I hope."

"*Why?*" the ceiling wondered.

"You should know. You know why. You've heard it all. You know it all."

"*Isn't there something else, anything else you could do? Is this your only choice? Are you sure you want to do this?*"

"I'm not sure of anything, of anything at all. That's the point. I couldn't think of anything else, and it's not that I didn't try. Believe me, I've been doing nothing else for quite awhile now. But, the harder I try, the longer I wait, the less I come up with, to the point where there's nothing. Absolutely nothing. And I can't stand it."

"*I'll miss you,*" the ceiling said mournfully.

I started to cry. "You'll be better off without me. Everybody will be better off without me."

Eventually, my sobs got softer and softer, light, irregular. My vision was blurry, and I was tired, sleepy. I became sort of numb, and while I had some awareness of where I was, it was almost like it was irrelevant to me. It was like slipping off into a dream, but at the same time, it was also different from a dream. I was in another place where it was just me and something else, but that something else was real confusing, real vague, kind of like, well, like time. Maybe that was it. How can I explain it? Well, in a dream, there's always a bit of fantasy, an internal question of "Is this really real?" which can be scary or reassuring, depending on what you're dreaming. This, however, was a feeling of transition, of change, of an ending. There was no question. There was no confusion. It just was. As I lay there, I started to bond with the feeling, to resign myself to it. It was like I was more than halfway down some long path with an end in sight, even though I couldn't make out the form or shape of the end. I just knew it was there, and I was OK with it, or at least I thought I was. It was a little late to start second-guessing, however. I was on my way. One-way ticket.

Just as I was starting to settle in, to feel like I'd arrived, something invaded my space. It was sort of distant, sort of surreal, and it was a thumping sound of some kind, like a knocking on a door. I heard a voice, but it, too, was distant. It didn't register, either. My peace was then shattered by this sudden screaming, and it upset me, disturbed my calm, and I wanted it to stop, to go away, but it wouldn't. The screaming just continued, and my tranquility was then further disturbed when I had a sensation of movement which seemed random and violent at first, like a sudden attack from an unknown assailant. All of this upset me, and I felt like my hiding place had been discovered, my secret passage exposed. I felt betrayed. Gradually, though, I recognized the voice, and it was that of my mother, but I couldn't make out what she was saying. I also came to realize that it was my shoulders that were being shaken, but I could not imagine why or what for. I just wanted it to stop. But, want it though I might, it just kept up.

After some time, I don't know how long, there were other voices, and they were all jumbled up, sometimes talking all at once, sometimes not. I could still hear the screaming voice, but it was quieter now, mingling with the others. There was a light flashed in my eyes, one at a time. There were other hands on me, and I was being lifted and placed on something, and then the sensation of movement. I felt cold and then heard slamming doors, and again lights in my eyes. Voices again, gibberish, confusing. Movement again, but faster, even more confusing.

Leave me alone! Go away! Let me be! I wanted to yell, but of course nothing would come out. Hands touching me, voices calling to me. And there wasn't a damn thing I could do about it. Once again, I was helpless, even when I tried to die. I couldn't do <u>anything</u> right! I was a failure in life, and I'm a failure at death. Loser to the bitter end. I gave up and let go, and it got darker, darker, and the sounds grew smaller, more distant, and melted into the background. The only sounds then were the ones in my own head:

> Yes, Jesus loves me.
> Yes, Jesus loves me.
> Yes, Jesus loves me.
> The Bible tells me so.

Fade to black.

CHAPTER 8

I don't know about death. I've thought about it a lot (obviously) but I must admit I really don't know much about it. How could I? Does anybody? Well, I suppose it's possible that doctors or funeral directors or something may have some kind of clue, as they see it frequently. Or how about, like, soldiers in a war? They must have some idea, as they are often on the giving and receiving end of death, so I'd imagine that they spend a decent amount of time reflecting on it. I mean, they are actually given the mission to kill or be killed. But me? I'm just a kid. Actually, I don't know much about anything at all, so I guess it would follow that I'm ignorant about the "Big One." But that sure hasn't kept me from reflecting on it, like how would it be to be dead. Would it be anything at all? If not, is that better than sticking with a shitty life? And, before someone gives me the "you don't know how lucky you are" speech, I admit that I'm not starving, or cold, or hungry. I know that, and actually I felt some guilt over that because I assume that anybody there would prefer to be me, but what can I tell you? There it is.

Death in the context of a religious belief also complicates things When you die, are you instantly "faxed" to the judgment, or is there some sort of scheduling thing that takes place, where you may not get in before the dead ahead of you? If so, where do you hang out while you're waiting? The Dead Lounge? Also, in our religion, suicide is kind of a big no-no, which could automatically keep you out of the pearly gates. However, I've had difficulty reconciling how God could create us to then have us feel like this. And while I look around at the world, there is more than enough misery to make one wonder how any kind of a compassionate creator could expect his (or her) creations to go through this stuff! If God could do this to us in this life, what if the Great Beyond turns out to merely be an eternal extension of the same thing? Or even worse? Any way you can guarantee me that's not the case? I didn't think so. So, to me, a lot of this heaven stuff is wishful thinking, because how could anybody make it through a single day without that hope? The entire planet could just fold up because life itself would be fundamentally absurd, the ultimate joke. I know the answers we were given in the religious education classes, and I can't say that there's not some appeal to that reasoning. I've tried to buy into it, to take it to heart, and most of the time I do. But, somehow, living in the pit, it didn't give me enough to keep the razor from my wrist. It's like discussing fire prevention strategies while the house burns down. A good idea but a little late. I needed a fire extinguisher.

Anyway, wherever I was I didn't stay, because I came to the slow realization that the sounds around me were voices that were decidedly human and not heavenly. "Molly," I heard from an unknown voice, "Can you hear me? Molly?" My level of awareness was limited because the sounds were initially something that were just there. I could hear, but it had no relevance. Slowly, though, I began to realize that the voice was directed at me.

Again, I heard it. "Molly?" I opened my eyes. The voice had a face, the face of a tall middle-age man with a stethoscope who was leaning over me. Not exactly the heavenly hosts. The voice continued, "Molly, do you know where you are?"

I shook my head.

"You are in the hospital. You cut your wrist. We're giving you blood to replace the blood you lost. There is an IV in your arm to do that. Do you understand?"

I nodded my head.

"Can you talk?"

"Yes," I said, and my voice surprised me. I sort of thought I'd heard the last of me.

"Good, good. My name is Dr. Lindson. Your family has been notified and they know you're here and that you're OK. We're going to monitor you for awhile to make sure everything is all right. In a little while another doctor will talk to you but all I want you to do now is rest. Do you understand that?"

"Yes," I said again.

"All right, then, I'll check back on you later on." He turned and left but this male nurse remained behind, busying himself about the room. I looked at my arm hanging from a suspended sling and the bag of blood dangling from a metal pole and followed the line of plastic tubing down to the IV needle that was inserted in my arm. The hospital giveth what Molly had taken away. Wonderful! I even screwed up my death. Can't do anything right. I laid there and wondered, what now? What the hell now? Living before death can be a big enough pain in the ass, but living after death? The hole was big, dark, and everywhere. It ached. It was a whole lot of nothing. The depression was a cloud that hung over me so I couldn't see, but that was OK. I didn't want to see.

I was sure that somewhere there was a clock ticking and time was going by, but it wasn't relevant to me as I laid there. Minutes were hours, hours were days, days were years. Who gave a damn? I was so disappointed in myself. The implosion was fairly complete, and I couldn't muster enough of anything to feel anything, anything at all. Does that make any sense? Is it possible to feel nothing? If it is, it must be just like that.

After a time in the vacuum, the door opened, the door closed, and somebody stood next to my bed, holding some sort of notebook. I turned my eyes ever so briefly in that direction, and then let them return to their starting position. Some middle-aged, nondescript woman of Oriental persuasion who was apparently here to talk to me. Whatever.

"Hello, Molly, I'm Dr. Ho."

Good for you.

"How are you?" Rhetorical questions are the worst. She pulled a chair over to the side of my bed and sat down, so I assumed we were going to be at this awhile. Wonderful. "Do you remember what happened? Do you know why you're here?"

I glanced briefly in her direction with an "Are you kidding?" look, but she felt obliged to clear it up anyway. "You tried to kill yourself by cutting your wrist. Your mother found you bleeding pretty badly and called an ambulance, and you were brought here. You had lost a lot of blood and needed a lot of stitches in your wrist. You also came real close to cutting the tendons but just nicked them. You're going to be OK."

Damn the luck.

"Was there something in particular that was bothering you bad enough that you tried to kill yourself? Something that happened?" I didn't respond. When it was clear I wasn't going to respond, she spoke again and said, "Molly, we want you to just rest for awhile, but obviously we're worried about you, and we're going to admit you here to the Crises Unit to make sure you're safe."

When I turned and looked in her direction in response to this news, she must have taken it as some form of communication. Gotta take what you can get.

"Look, Molly, if your mom hadn't found you, it's likely that you wouldn't be here now. It's clear that there are a number of things that are hurting you, and you need to take the time to figure out what those things are. We're not going to take a chance with your life. Do you understand? Does that make sense to you?"

Again with the rhetorical questions.

"Also, Molly, you should know that it's common to be even more depressed after a suicide attempt than you were before. I'm going to prescribe some medication to help with

122

that. It takes awhile for it to take full effect, though, so I don't want you surprised when you don't notice anything right away. OK?"

I nodded.

"Your moods are likely to be all over the place right now, and they can go from bad to worse, but that's not unusual, and we'll help you with that. It's really important that you start to trust someone, and we're here only to help. I know you don't really know us yet, but you will.

Your parents are obviously real concerned about you, and there's been calls from your friends from school asking how you're doing, but we think it's a good idea that you deal with some of these feelings of yours before you get any company."

Actually, most of me welcomed that. I mean, what exactly would I say? "Oh, me? Those stitches? Oh, that's nothing. I just tried to kill myself but you know how that goes! A whole lot of blood but no dead." I don't think so.

"So, here's what will happen. Medically, you're recovering well. You'll be transferred to the Crises Unit in a day or so where you'll probably have a roommate. In the Unit, you'll be involved in therapy where you talk with me and the counselors individually, you talk in groups with other kids who are on the Unit, too, and you talk in family therapy, too."

Hearing that, I winced.

"Is that a problem, Molly?" the doctor asked, as she must have noticed my editorial expression.

I shrugged my shoulders. I didn't want to let any more cats out of the bag or she might give my mother the empty bed in the room but, holy shit! Family therapy? "Would that include my father?" I inquired, knowing the answer before it came out of her mouth.

"It will involve whoever it needs to involve, but don't worry about that now." She smiled softly, reached out and gently put her hand on my shoulder. What could I say? I was what they call a captive audience, but the thought of all of us sitting around together swapping family stories made me shake, and I struggled to subdue it. "You just get well and I'll see you when you come on the Unit" and she left.

My male nurse-guard-babysitter came back on duty and I put my head back on the pillow and gazed up. Doing so, I realized that not any ceiling would do, and I was not bonded with the suspended variety hovering over me in this drab hospital room, a total stranger. No friends. No friends at all. I started to reflect on a potential parental powwow but I could get but only so far. Way too strange, way too scary, way too surreal. This doctor would have to be a witch-doctor, or a sadist, or some damn thing to bring my family together. Oil and water, or Steven and Margaret, don't mix.

If that wasn't enough, I also realized I hadn't thought much of Craig since I got here, but I did then. I was sure he knew by then. Sure he knew that his girlfriend was a head-case, a goddamn suicidal loony who kissed and then cut. I felt humiliated when I thought of it, and I felt awful that I was putting the poor kid through this. He never did anything but care for me, and this was the thanks he got. I wondered who told him. I wondered what he was told. I wondered what he must have thought when he heard. I wondered how I could ever face him again. I wondered if I ever would.

I lifted my left arm and looked at the wrist I slashed, and it was covered with gauze. I waited until the nurse was distracted a bit, pulled up the gauze, and peeked at the wound. It was an ugly sucker, my best to date, long, jagged red, pissed-off, with white string tied up in tight little knots where the stitches were. I let it go as the nurse turned in my direction. Failure in life, failure in death.

One thing's for sure in a hospital room - there's a whole lot of nothing to do, especially when you can't have visitors. I flipped through the TV channels with the remote, but it was merely an exercise in wasting time, something I was quite good at. A rerun here, a game show there, followed by a little trash TV, and none of it made the least bit of sense to me. It was noise, colors, and people with no point, but I didn't care. I was just staring, just killing time. (Oops, sorry.) I wondered about the medication Dr. Ho prescribed and when it would start helping, because the only thing I felt now was tired, tired and lost. Tired and sad. Tired and overwhelmed.

I spent the rest of the day dozing on and off, mostly because there was nothing else to do, and partly I think because of the medication, which made me sleepy. In between, I reflected on the awful reality that I actually tried to kill myself and judging by the size of the scar on my wrist, I must have come close. I could be dead, but I wasn't. I could be free, but I wasn't. I could be in heaven, or in hell, or in some kind of eternal nothingness, but I wasn't. And why? Was I meant to live, or just too incompetent to complete the act?

And what about my family? What in the name of God were they thinking? What was I going to tell them? What was there to be said? And my friends at school, and everybody else there, what about them? How could I ever face them again? The thoughts just came like some kind of scary stampede, and I gave up trying to control them. Screw ya! Go ahead, have a ball. Anyway, I deserved the pain.

The sun went down and my dinner arrived and I nibbled at it for appearances sake with my nurse friend who was still lurking around, but I wasn't sure if it was getting me any points. He took my blood pressure, temperature, etc., at different times, scribbling the data on a chart. I noticed a name tag on his shirt that told me his name was Mark.

At some point, another nurse came and had a chitchat with my escort, and he returned to the room, obviously with some news to share as he walked over to the side of my bed. "Molly, Dr. Lindson said you should be all right to travel now, so we're going to be moving you up to the Crises Unit now, all right?"

I didn't think I was in a position to decline the offer. "OK, Mark."

He removed my IV, gathered up the minimal stuff I had in the room, including the clothes I came in with, and wheeled in a wheelchair to the side of my bed.

"Hop on," he said brightly, and I sat up and swung my legs over the side of the bed. I hadn't done much with the exception of going to the bathroom a couple of times, and I was still anything but perky, but I was OK, at least physically.

I stood up with the nurse's assistance, which was more symbolic than needed, and he maneuvered the wheelchair underneath me. I dropped into the chair and we were rolling, out the door and down the hall. We passed various rooms with various folks in varying degrees of disrepair on my way, and I wondered about their stories in this "House of Pain." We hung a left at the end of the hall aiming for the elevators, and boarded the next shuttle for whatever awaited on the 5th floor, as the nurse pushed and lit up the number 5 on the elevator panel. Small talk was nonexistent on this trip, which fortunately did not include any additional passengers along the way and, after docking, the nurse motored me out the door, down another hall, and through a pair of double doors innocently labeled "Phelps - 5", whatever the hell that meant. There was some kind of desk/nurses' station ahead, and he stopped when we got there to register me with the "clerk." It wasn't like checking into the Holiday Inn, and I guess I didn't need to worry about a reservation. I hoped I'd get a room with a view of the garden. Heck, I hoped they had a garden. The woman behind the counter came out, and she walked over to me with my nurse escort.

"Hi, Molly, my name is Susan Doud. I'm a social worker here on Phelps. How are you?" Ms. Doud was relatively young (and relatively big!) with short, curly light hair and an animated expression that seemed like it should be out of place for this kind of place. She was also dressed in jeans and a sweatshirt that seemed more appropriate for a mall instead of a hospital. She really did seem to be more of a greeter than a jailer, and she appeared genuinely happy to have me as a visitor. I wasn't exactly jumping on the Welcome Wagon yet, however, and I mumbled some monosyllables in her direction. "Well, good, good," she answered enthusiastically, like she had actually deciphered my drivel. I'm glad she knew what I said, because I sure didn't. "We're going to take you to your room now, OK?"

Whatever. My escort, Mark, leaned over in my direction. "Molly, I'm going to go now. Good luck. You're in good hands here." I weakly waved good-bye with my good arm. It was a short relationship, and a strange one at that.

Ms. Doud told me, "You can ditch that wheelchair, now, Molly. It's just hospital policy to move you in one of those."

"Oh, good," I answered and stood, feeling a bit wobbly at first but not bad. Ms. Doud moved closer to me in a precautionary stance while I worked at regaining my balancing skills, teetering to the left and right a bit just to test the system, and I passed the drill as I didn't fall down.

"I'll show you your room and introduce you to your roommate. We also called your parents and asked them to bring in some of your clothes, and they're in the room."

"OK."

"Also, after you've settled into your room, I'll come and talk to you a little about what you can expect while you're here, and answer any questions you might have that I can answer. Some of them, though, may need to be asked to Dr. Ho. Oh, and if you were wondering, you can call me Susan. We try not to be too formal, OK?"

I nodded.

"Follow me, then." She started to walk down this corridor and I walked behind her, and she paused every few steps to make sure I didn't vaporize, or beam out, or something. We walked past various rooms that were obviously of the hospital variety, but they'd been modified to look more "homey," if that was even remotely possible under the circumstances. There were kids here and there in some of the rooms, and some paused briefly as we walked by, but they all quickly resumed whatever they were doing, like talking or reading. We passed a bigger, open area that must have been a game room of some type as there was a Ping-Pong table, a television with a couch and some chairs around it, various magazines in a rack, and a few tables. There were a few kids in there watching the tube, reading, and playing cards at the tables. That was cool. I hadn't seen anybody actually play cards in a long time unless it was Solitaire on the computer. Actually, now that I thought of it, you didn't see anybody do much of <u>anything</u> that required honest-to-god, face-to-face, human-to-human interaction anymore. "In-person" had been replaced by "on-line."

We turned down another hall and walked a bit before Susan stopped in front of a room labeled 524. "OK, Molly, this is your room," she said, gesturing inside. I caught up to her and turned into the room where another girl sat on one of the two beds inside. She was just kind of sitting there staring blankly and looked up briefly as I entered, offering me a meek smile. "Samantha, this is your new roommate, Molly. Molly, this is Samantha." The girl gave me some kind of a wave by lifting and wiggling her fingers a bit.

"Hi," she said.

"Hi," I answered, giving an equally wimpy wave.

"Samantha's been here for a little while," Susan explained, "and she can probably answer some questions for you about where stuff is and how we do things. I'll also talk to you after you settle in and answer any questions you might have. It may be a little confusing to you at first but you'll get used to the routines pretty quickly. There will be different staff here at different times and you can talk to any of them at any time but I'll be what we call your Primary Therapist, so I'll be your main source of information. If you need something, or have any problems, you can always ask any of the staff but I'll be your main source of information and you can always come to me or ask anyone to let me know you need to talk to me. All right?"

"Sure," I said, although it wasn't true because I really had no idea what to expect, but I also had no idea what to ask. Susan proceeded to give me some other basic information, such as where my clothes were, where the bathrooms were, the kitchenette area, and some of the basic rules, e.g., no leaving the unit, no smoking (although I had no idea how one would get a cigarette anyway), etc. She explained that communication to family, friends, and so on was restricted at first because I needed time to get used to the routines on the Unit and because I'd benefit from some time without the pressures I must have been experiencing. Susan seemed like a nice enough woman, and she had a friendly but very direct way of sharing information, like looking me right in the eyes at the end of her sentences and asking "OK?" at the end of each one, pausing to wait until I answered.

"I'll give you two a chance to get to know each other for awhile, and you can rest a bit if you want to, Molly. OK?"

"Sure."

"All right, then. I'll see you in a little while."

Susan then turned and left, and I was alone with my new roommate. It was as awkward as hell at first, as I had no clue what to say, and apparently Samantha didn't either, as she continued to sit on her bed, looking around the room with obvious discomfort. I shuffled over to what was now my bed, pulled the pillow up and fluffed it against the backboard before climbing up on the bed and leaning back against the pillow. I suddenly realized I was beat from my little jaunt to the Unit, and my shoulders sagged as I settled into this position. My legs felt tingly from the exertion, and I stretched them out in front of me on the bed. The silence was loud as we both sat there, waiting for someone to crack. I figured I was new here, and I wasn't going first! Finally, after an eternity, the tension was like a stretched piano wire before Samantha coughed, and she turned and smiled at me from the obviousness of it, and we both laughed a little. The nervous meter went down twenty or thirty degrees. "Sorry," she said with a voice sorta deep and husky for a girl.

"That's OK," I answered. There! Ice broken!

"What are you in for?" Samantha whispered with comical convict coyness. I held up my bandaged wrist for her to see, and she smiled and said "Ah, the old slashed wrist. A very popular choice around here."

"How about you?" I asked, as it seemed only polite to inquire about her admission ticket.

"Eatin' and barfing," she responded with dramatic flair. "Chewin' and chuckin." I gave her a puzzled look and she said, "Bulimia, if you want the technical term, but I think that sounds so stuffy, don't you?" I just shrugged my shoulders. "Haven't thought much about it?"

I shrugged the shoulders again.

"I don't blame you," she said, "It's actually quite a disgusting problem. Not at all romantically spooky, like depression, although they tell me I've got a touch of that, too."

"How long have you been here?"

"For almost four days, but whose counting? Four days this time, that is."

"So you've been here before?"

"A couple of times. They do what they can, I suck up and tell them what they want to hear, and out the door I go. I'm afraid this time, though, I might have pushed it too far. There's been talk of me being moved to an eating disorders clinic out of town. That'll be a real hoot, don't you think?" I was having a hard time telling if this girl was really excited about this or just being dramatic, but I sensed it was the latter. "And how about you? What has you trying to bite the big one?" This girl didn't seem prone to subtlety.

"I don't know," I answered more honestly than not.

"Is this your first time?"

"My first time what?" I asked, uncertain of her request.

"Your first time here."

"Oh! Yeah, it's my first. I haven't been here before."

"Well, welcome to what we affectionately refer to as the Zoo. I'm sure you'll feel at home with all the other exotic animals we have on display."

"How many kids are here?" I wondered, as a head count was hard to take while walking down the hall.

"It varies," she said, "but it's usually around twenty-five or so, except when there's a full moon. We're usually at capacity then." Again, it was difficult to tell if she was just jazzing me or if she was serious, but I was beginning to suspect that Samantha didn't do serious. As I looked at her, it was difficult to see Sam as what I mentally associated with the term "eating disorder." I mean, she was what you might kindly call "sturdy" in her stature, with significant shoulders and an overall thickness in her upper body that could be mistaken for male if you looked at her quickly from behind. She was tall, too, around six feet or more, I was guessing. She seemed to move awkwardly, like someone who was embarrassed to be there, trying to avoid detection, which almost guarantees getting noticed. As she moved about the room, she stayed in a hunched posture with her big shoulders curved to form an uncomfortable looking bow in her back. "This is your dresser here," she said, pointing at a nondescript set of drawers just opposite the spare bed I assumed was mine as she was lying on the other one.

"Thanks."

"There's some stuff in it already. One of the aides brought some clothes in here before and put them in the drawers. They ask your family to bring some stuff in when you're coming. You do have a family, don't you?"

I grimaced. "Kinda."

"What do you mean, 'kinda'? Either you got a family or you don't."

"It's a long story."

Sam just rolled her eyes and then her big shoulders. "Aren't they all? We've got a lot of 'long stories' around here. Believe me, you'll get your chance to tell yours soon enough."

"I can't wait."

It got sort of quiet after this brief bonding exchange. I just sat on what was now my bed, looking uncomfortably around the room, scoping out my new digs while Sam returned to leafing through whatever magazine she had (which I deeply hoped was anything but "People.") The room was painted some sort of green that gave the term "dull" new meaning. There was a window in the room that had those kind of blinds that are built right into the window and no curtains, which I assumed was to prevent us from hanging ourselves with a curtain cord, but someone had painted some sort of floral design around the window frame. Very homey! Each of the dressers had an attached mirror, and I stood up and walked over to check out my look. It was me, all right, but I was definitely far from ready for prime-time. I had the appropriately confused appearance of someone who had tried to do one's self in and was now in the Looney Hotel, which I decided was not a good look for me, I can tell you. I made brief eye-contact with me, sneered, and turned to the window.

I looked out the window at the parking lot below, and watched a couple of cars pull out and a couple of cars pull in. The last one came in real quick, and I watched this guy jump out and go around to the passenger side where a woman who was quite obviously pregnant was starting to get out of the car. He hustled to get the door for her, and she rose and started to walk while he grabbed her arm to support her. Together, they walked into the Emergency Room entrance that was there with her door still open and the car still running. Less than a minute or two later, the guy reappeared, closed her door, and jumped in the car, moving it to an open parking spot a bit away in the parking lot. He jumped out again, this time with a suitcase in his hand. He trotted, almost ran, back into the Emergency Room with the suitcase swinging wildly as he ran. It all looks so neat at the beginning, doesn't it? A big adventure. It made me sad, and I turned and walked back to the bed.

"What time is it?" I asked Samantha.

"I don't know. Kinda late."

"How late can you stay up in here?"

"They want lights off at about 11:00 o'clock. Most kids just hang out watching TV, or sit in their rooms and read, or just hang out and talk. I usually just stay in here. I've done this enough that all the novelty's warn off. I'm all talked out."

"What do you do in here all night?"

Samantha just broadly extended both her arms and smiled. "You're lookin' at it," she said. I sighed, and Sam asked, "You were expecting some kind of club atmosphere?"

"No, I really didn't know what to expect, actually. I haven't done this before."

"You first-timers are such babes in the woods. Well, don't worry, kid. If you stick with me, you'll be a polished pro in no time."

"I can hardly wait." I considered wandering out into the main area and seeing what was up but decided I wasn't up for all the chitchat it would entail. I just laid there, trying to acquaint myself with yet another ceiling, trying to get to know each other, but it was hard with Sam there. After all, these relationships needed nurturing, some quality time, some getting to know each other, and it was hard with another person there. It was all too new, and we were all strangers. Two's company, three's a crowd, and all that. So, I just laid there, breathing in, breathing out. I couldn't figure out what the proper thing to think was, so I thought about that. I couldn't decide what the proper thing to do was, so I thought about that, too. After some time passed while I pondered these pointless points, Susan came back into the room.

"So, how you doing so far?" Susan asked, sitting on a chair that was by the side of my bed.

"Fine."

"Are you settling in?"

"Uh-huh."

"How about I take you out and show you around the place? I can introduce you to the other kids."

"I'd rather not tonight, if that's all right with you. I'm really tired, and I'd just as soon go to sleep."

She smiled. "All right. I'm sure it was a real long day for you, and not an easy one, either. You have pajamas and other stuff you need in the dresser, and you can change into whatever you want. You also have a bathroom bag your folks put together with your toothbrush, toothpaste, shampoo, and other stuff you'll need. We'll bring whatever medication you need to take to you, or call you out to for it when you're familiar with the routines." She turned to Samantha and said, "Can you help Molly out if she has any questions about where everything is, Samantha?"

"Sure," Samantha said.

"OK, then. I'll see you guys tomorrow. Sleep tight, and don't let the bedbugs bite!" Susan waved goodnight and left.

"Is she that corny all the time?" I asked my roomie.

"Uh, yes. All the time, as a matter of fact. She's pretty nice, though. You get used to her bad jokes."

"I can't wait." It was quiet and awkward again, and small talk was real hard to come by. It really can be uncomfortable trying to share personal space with somebody you don't know, and it was particularly hard under conditions where what you had in common was being mutually screwed-up. I tossed and turned on my bed and tried to mentally acclimate to this room, this bed, this girl, this whole damn situation, and it wasn't easy, I'll tell you. Not that long ago, I was home, and now I was here, a psycho prisoner. However, I've felt like a prisoner for a long time so I guess it was more like just changing correctional facilities. Kinda like being transferred to maximum security.

"Do you want to go to sleep?" Sam asked. I guess my silence was sending signals.

"Oh, sorry. Am I being a pain?"

"Look, girlfriend, compared to some of my previous roommates, you're a walk in the park so far. There was this girl, Charice, who was here before you. She was a real piece of work. She would not shut up! She talked all day, she talked all night, she talked while she was brushing her teeth, for Christ's sake. She drove me nuts! You can lay there and stare at the wall all day if you want. That's just fine with me."

"I just didn't want you to think I was being rude, or anything."

"Hey, Molly, this isn't a sorority. If you want to talk, talk. If you don't want to talk, don't. I'm not your goddamn Brownie leader." I could see this girl had a hard time sharing emotions!

"Sorry," I said, and she gave me this look that said say that again and I'll rip your lungs out. I waved my hand to let her know I got the nonverbal message and rolled over. Sam got up and turned off the light and settled into her bed. I laid there with my eyes wide open and stared at the wall next to my bed. It can be so weird to sleep in a strange place and in a strange bed, but you should try this out. While it was generally quiet outside the room, there was still a sliver of light under the door and occasional sounds of people using a bathroom, some muffled talk down the hall where the "graveyard shift" (no pun intended) must hang out, and a pervasive sense of being a stranger in a building full of strangers. I was a bit groggy from what I assumed was the medication, but it was still hard to sleep. It was all too weird. Sam, on the other hand, was snoring like my brother in only a few minutes or so, and it helped to know I was alone in the room, at least from a consciousness standpoint.

I rolled over and looked up. While we were still unacquainted, the ceiling and I had at least gotten past the uncomfortable preliminaries in our relationship. We were in the "feeling each other out" stage, sizing each other up. *"So, how's it going?"* I was asked.

"How does it <u>look</u> like it's going?"

"Sorry. I didn't mean to sound stupid."

"Hey, when it comes to sounding stupid, you're talking to the queen. Also, for your information, I own the 'sorry' word. I have <u>all</u> the copyrights."

"OK, sorry."

I glared.

"Oops," the ceiling said sheepishly. Suddenly, I knew we would get along famously. We had <u>so</u> much in common. I drifted off to sleep, followed by dreams of Mom, and Dad, and Craig, and various combinations and permutations of the three. I wouldn't exactly call it restful or refreshing but, what the hell, it never really is. I certainly didn't expect the sandman to stop by with his "A" game here. And, one thing I can always count on is never being able to count on anything.

CHAPTER 9

I suppose they would have awakened me if I didn't wake up on my own, but that wasn't a particular problem this morning. I opened my eyes at a time that had to be early as it looked just a little less dark outside but far from light yet. You know, that time when it's hard to tell if it's more day than night, when the black turns to gray and then dull silver with bright edges that rim the outline of sky versus earth. When yesterday is more gone than here, but today really hasn't arrived yet. It's that tug-of-war that light always wins, even though it looks like the odds are about fifty-fifty at first. As always, the sun slowly crept up and the darkness slithered away. It was difficult to tell if they were companions or competitors in the never-ending role-playing game but, eventually and inevitably, the light took over and the noise level slowly increased all around with more traffic noise, shuffling feet in the hallway, and voices that grew less and less timid and subdued. I wondered what the day ahead would bring, but I suspected it would be interesting. Samantha was still snoring away, and it looked like fun, although a bit noisy.

I reached over to my watch and pushed the button to light up the digital face, and it was 7:49. The thought occurred to me that winter wouldn't even start for almost another two weeks and we'd yet to face the darkest day. Well, at least astronomically, that is.

I was guessing that we had about ten minutes before somebody rained on our parade and, indeed, a woman I didn't know stuck her head inside the door and said, "Girls, time to get up. Let's go." She stood there for a moment while Sam continued to snooze. "Samantha," she said, this time with more emphasis. She then turned to me and said, "Hi" with a smile. I waved and smiled back. Sam wearily opened an eye in her direction, like a slumbering lion at a zoo who's being pestered by the public. "Let's go," she said again and then slipped out, closing the door with authority on her way out. Sam assumed her previous position, and I wondered if she was going to ignore the obvious mandate to, uh, "rise and shine." Before I had time to consider what the staff's next tactic would be in such a situation, however, Sam groaned, rolled and almost fell out of the bed. Her eyes glanced right over me as she rose and tried to stand straight, but it's like I wasn't even there. She made it to about 80 degrees vertical or so and must have decided that was close enough as she lumbered into the bathroom. After an extended period of silence, when she was doing God-knows-what in there, I heard a shower running.

I figured my options were limited as well and I got up, feeling suprisingly nimble considering the circumstances. I think it was still a combination of adrenaline and anxiety, but the buzz was OK with me. There was a sink and mirror in a corner of the room, so I walked over, taking my bathroom bag from my dresser with me. I splashed cold water on my face and brushed my teeth, carefully avoiding my mirror image. I opened my dresser and picked out a day's wardrobe, surprised at the positive clothing choices made by my mother. On the other hand, she didn't exactly have a wide variety to choose from style-wise as the Skater look is somewhat limited. Samantha eventually emerged from the bathroom, looking a whole-lot better in a bathrobe with her dark brown hair still wet and hanging just down to her shoulders, combed through but not styled in any way. "It's all yours," she said, pointing to the bathroom. "Hurry up while there's still hot water."

"Thanks." I went in and showered, brushed back my hair, and plastered on some minimal make-up. Walking back in the room, I faced the sudden timidity that comes when you have to dress in front of a stranger. I dawdled around the room trying to work up the nerve to change but eventually just scooped up my clothes and went back into the bathroom to put them on. I was uncomfortable enough around others fully clothed; I sure wasn't ready to parade around in my skivvies.

I walked back out and Sam teased, "Bit of a prude, are we?"

I was briefly miffed as I thought we weren't familiar enough for such a personal comment yet but then decided, what the hell! "Yes, we are."

"Hey, don't worry about it. That's fine with me. I'm not exactly what you could call an exhibitionist, either." She smiled, and I felt a bit more relaxed. "If you're ready, I'll escort you out to breakfast," and pointed theatrically at the door. I nodded and she walked out the door with me in tow.

We walked down the hall to the dining area I'd passed yesterday on the way in, and there were already a bunch of kids sitting there eating and others who were getting food from serving trays that were set up against a wall. It was what you would call an "eclectic" gathering of varying genders, ages, sizes, and hair colors (some God-given, some chemically-given). Kids looked up with that "Who's the new kid?" look but promptly returned to breakfast as usual.

Sam picked up a tray and said, "Grab what you want and come on over here," nodding to a particular table where two other girls were sitting. I picked up a tray but stood there, following Sam's lead. She grabbed some pancakes, some toast, and some juice before saddling up at the table. I just took some cereal and a container of milk and went to sit down, but Sam called out, "What? No juice?" I don't know why but I reached over and put some orange juice on my tray. Sam smiled at me and said, "Good. Ya gotta get your vitamins!"

I placed my tray on the table and sat down as Samantha announced, "Guys, this is Molly, our newest inmate. Molly, these are your fellow sheep." There were a couple of awkward hellos from the other girls and I mumbled back the same. After a few uncomfortable mouthfuls and moments,

Sam said, "Oh, shit! Where are my manners? Molly, this is Erica and Joline. They've been here almost as long as me BUT NOT as often as me." We repeated our hellos before returning to eating. "Molly's in for the suicidal slash. Show'em your work, Molly."

I squirmed a bit before Joline said, "That's OK, Molly. Don't listen to her. Sam loves an audience. You don't need to show us. Does she, Erica?"

Looking disgusted, Erica said, "Actually, Molly, we'd prefer you didn't. When you've seen one slashed wrist, you've seen them all," and with that she held up her own arm, revealing scars all up and down from her elbow to her hand.

"Jeez, and I thought I was <u>so</u> cutting edge," I said, and everybody cracked up. Yes, I can be witty from time to time. At that moment, I felt like I passed the induction exam, and I was then much more at ease. We talked and laughed, and I even managed to get in a few more one-liners before breakfast ended. I was about ready to ask what happens next when Susan came in and walked over to our table.

"Did you figure out how to get fed?" Susan asked me.

"I showed her the way," Sam jumped in.

"Thanks, Sam," Susan said condescendingly. "So, you doing OK, Molly?"

"Yeah, Sam's been a big help," and with that Sam broke out in a broad smile. The other girls looked at each other with knowing grins.

"Well, thanks again, Sam," Susan said while Samatha continued with her look of accomplishment. Susan turned to me and said, "I need to chat with you for a little while, Molly."

"Oh, OK, sure. Now?"

"If you don't mind. If you're done eating."

"No, that'll be fine. Now is fine," and I stood up. Susan walked away, motioning to me to follow her, which I did.

We walked out of the dining area and down another hall which had office-looking setups in each room. Susan paused when she reached one, saying, "C'mon in here, Molly, and have a seat." I strolled in and dropped into the obvious "guest" chair on one side of the desk while Susan sat in the other "owner" one. Her office seemed typical (at least in my to my experience to date) but what stood out to me were the family pictures scattered about, with portraits of two little boys and a girl who looked about ten or so in addition to a man I assumed was the father, as he was in many of the pictures.

Susan must have noticed me checking out her family. "Do you like my pictures?" She asked.

"What? Oh, yes, they're real nice. Are they your children?"

"Yes, they are."

"How old are they?"

"Jessica is the oldest, she's eleven. Francis is seven and Harrison is six. That's my husband, Jack."

"The kids are cute."

"Thanks. I think so, too."

"Where's their Dad?"

"Do you mean are we still married?"

Embarrassed, I said, "Yeah. Sorry, I guess that wasn't the best way to put it."

Susan smiled and said, "That's all right, Molly. Don't worry about that. And yes, we are <u>still</u> married."

"That's nice."

Susan smiled again and said, "Yes, Molly. It is nice." Changing the subject (thank God!), Susan asked, "So, how are you doing so far? Are you and Sam getting to know each other?"

"Yeah, she's kind of funny."

"That she is, that she is. How about the medication? Are you doing all right with that?"

"I think it makes me a bit tired, but it's not too bad. Should I be feeling anything else?"

"Well, don't look to it as the answer but it can help. Think of it as a support, OK?"

"OK."

Susan then explained some of the routines of the Unit, such as individual therapy, group therapy with others on the Unit, and the one I was looking forward to, family therapy. I must have had some kind of knee-jerk reaction to those last two words because, just like Dr. Ho, Susan asked, "You're not wild about that idea, Molly?"

"Not particularly."

"Trust me, you'll survive. I'll be there to help all of you during the sessions." Susan explained how it usually went in some detail, and I felt a bit more at ease with the idea but far from relaxed. I knew it was going to happen, and even knew it needed to happen, but I was far from psyched about it. I think we even started the individual therapy right then as she talked with me about my background and some of the situations that were stressing me, including the family stuff, school, and friends. We touched a bit on the session I had with Dr. Raimes, and I let her know we only had one before I ended up in the hospital. "Do you think you'll want to continue with him after you leave here?" Susan asked.

"You mean you think I'll get out?"

Susan chuckled and said, "Well, we don't plan on raising you here, Molly. Yes, I think you'll get out. I told you when you first got here, this is a short-term thing."

"Oh, that's good."

"Yes, I think it is."

"I wouldn't mind going back to him. He was a nice guy."

"Good. You need to be hooked up with somebody before you leave. You can't think that the problems that led you to try to kill yourself are minor enough that a brief visit here will be all you need. Look at this as a beginning, or at least a foundation, for starting to get at all that's bugging you, but plan on staying at it for the near future. OK?"

"Yeah."

"Also, I'd like to talk to Dr. Raimes if that's all right with you. We'll give you what's called a Release of Information for you and your parents to sign that gives us and him permission to talk to each other. We can then plan for what you need when you're going back home. We have some others, too, but we'll get to them when we get to them. OK?

"Yeah, that's fine."

"Great!" We talked some more about this and that, and she told me I could go back to my room. I'd be going to my first group session in a little while, and there was also school work that I'd be doing as they checked with my school to find out what I was working on and had my parents bring in my books and stuff. Susan then walked me back to my room where I joined up with Sam who was talking with Joline and Erica. They asked me how I was doing, and they both seemed genuinely concerned about me, which I thought was nice. Sam, in particular, seemed to take me under her wing. She kept telling me to let her know if anything or anybody bothered me because "I know my way around here." It was sort of sweet, actually, because I never had a big sister to look out for me. Come to think of it, I'm not sure if there was ever anybody who'd ever really looked out for me. Sort of a weird place and way to find it, don't you think?

Joline, with her short-cropped, brunette hair and wire-rimmed round glasses hiding gentle brown eyes, was kind of cute but in a plain kind of way. Slender and small, she seemed sort of quiet, certainly in comparison to Sam, but she was nice. She spent most of the time just laughing at Sam's many jokes, but she did talk. When she did, she was actually pretty witty herself, with a sharp tongue subtly and dryly delivered. For example, when Sam was talking about some of the staff, Joline would quietly interrupt her and ask something like, "Oh, you mean Mother Superior" or "You would be referring to Nurse Ratchet?" (whoever she was) or "That would be the Grim Reaper" (he sounded nice). I had no idea who these people were but Joline must have been somewhat on target as Sam cracked up with each biting line.

Erica, on the other hand, had all the physical positives going for her. She had a nice figure packaged in a tall frame with long shining brown hair and blue eyes that absolutely glistened. Her jeans were casual but perfect, and her red turtleneck sweater was a great match with her long neck and a light complexion that I seriously doubt ever dealt with a zit. Looking at her, I wondered what could have caused her admission to this place. On the outside, she seemed relatively self-assured, but then I'd seen the scars on her arm. I guess looks can be deceiving in a lot of different ways. She seemed like she could be the living example of what my English teacher defined as an oxymoron, like "jumbo shrimp," except with Erica it was "beautiful head-case." She also had a mouth that was <u>way</u> out of place with her homecoming queen exterior. She was able to work the word "fuck" into just about every sentence in a multitude of creative combinations that would make a vulgar novelist proud. For example, in addition to the ever-popular phrases such as "fuck that," "fucking pain in the ass," and "what the fuck," she came up with some new twists including "abso-fucking-lutely" and my personal favorite, "hoop-ti-fucking--do." While I was a bit taken back at first when I heard her ripping the "F" word out so prolifically, after awhile it was just another word, she used it so much. Also, she was so statuesque and she dropped the word so casually it almost sounded good coming from her in her leading lady voice.

While I mostly listened rather than talked during this chitchat session with my fellow loonies, there was one thing I was wondering and after awhile I asked, "Hey, girls, where are the guys?" They looked at me funny, so I clarified. "Boys! There are boys in this place, too, aren't there? I saw some when I was first brought in here."

"Why?" Sam teased. "Are you interested?"

"No," I said, a bit embarrassed and somewhat defensive. "But I saw them, so what's the deal?"

They were smirking a bit but I think they basically believed me. Joline explained, "They join us in Group and we share the Recreation Areas but their rooms are separate. They keep real good tabs on that."

"Oh," I said.

"That's it?" Erica said.

"What do you mean, 'that's it'?"

"I mean, do you want to know anything else?"

"No."

"OK, then." They all looked at each other with not even thinly veiled skepticism but they dropped it anyway. I didn't feel like explaining that I had a guy, or at least I think I had a guy, or was on my way to getting a guy, or some damn thing. Anyway, I didn't know what the hell the status of that was at the moment, and after all it was only one freaking date, so it seemed better to just let it be. Besides, I'd just met these girls and while they seemed nice I was not at all ready to stick my neck out in that way. I've been burned before, thank you very much.

Just about then, somebody in the hall called out loudly, "Time for Group." The girls got up and Sam looked over and said "Let's move it, rookie. Front and center!" The others chuckled as I hustled to catch up with them, and I followed as they walked past the nurses' station (or whatever it was) and down another hall before hanging a left into another room. Susan was standing just outside the room and made eye contact with me, smiling. "Welcome, Molly. So Sam showed you the way.?"

"Piece of cake," I answered.

"Well, stroll on in. I'll be there in a minute." Other kids were already in the room and some were standing and talking and a few were sitting in the chairs already. Again, there were some glances in my direction and a bit of muffled talk which I assumed, paranoid that I am, had to be about the "new kid," but I'd be curious, too, if I was an old-timer. I just shadowed Sam who seemed happy to lead me by the nose. It reminded me of what the Biology teacher had described as a "symbiotic relationship," like a shark and a lamprey eel, and I had latched on with all my tentacles (or whatever the hell that disgusting creature uses to hang on for the ride.) Samantha sat down and I did, too, in the chair next to hers.

"OK, kids, let's get going," Susan said, and everybody grabbed a seat, and there was a total of ten including us. "As I'm sure you've all noticed, we have a newcomer. Everybody, say hello to Molly." A mixed chorus of hi's and hello's went up with a few waves. "I'd like all of you to introduce yourselves. Eric, let's begin with you," Susan said, turning to a boy just to her left.

"Hi. As you just heard and as you <u>must</u> have already known, I'm Eric," and everyone laughed a little. He was your basic burner - hair shaved on one side and hanging long and straight on the other, head-banging group photo on his black tee-shirt, baggy pants almost falling off his butt.

"Hi, Eric," I said. The rest of the group then took turns and I met the boys I hadn't met, including Philip, a tall, skinny redhead; Harlan, a short, stocky and serious-looking guy; and Justin, another stoner-looking type with green and purple hair and a <u>seriously</u> pierced body. I was also reintroduced to the girls I had already met. Susan explained the group rules, primarily for my benefit, I believe, as I was the only new kid, and she then sort of opened the floor for discussion. A number of interesting topics were discussed and a variety of interesting reactions elicited, ranging from light laughter to big-time anger with a generous helping of anxieties, disinterest, and disappointments in between. A particularly popular topic appeared to be the holidays, which were fast approaching. It started with Justin making some disparaging crack about the absence of thanks in Thanksgiving and that apparently lit a fuse that burned hot and quick among the group.

"I <u>hate</u> the holidays!" Justin said, "I freaking hate them! I wish I could go out of the country or something until January 2nd. I can't <u>wait</u> until they're over," a sentiment that was almost universally shared by this group judging by the comments that followed Justin's declaration.

"What is it about the holidays that you guys dislike so much?" Susan asked.

"What's there to like?" Erica said. "Everybody sits around and tries to act like they're all having a good time and all anybody really wants to do is get out the door as fast as possible. It's all such a farce. We start off with this one big happy family bullshit but by the time the turkey's carved, everybody's ready to cut each other's throats instead of the pumpkin pie." She paused, breathing a bit heavy, and then started again, with the words just tumbling out. She was staring down at the floor and I don't know who in particular she was talking to, but I wasn't sure it was any of us. "Like, I remember two years ago when my father and brother got into it over some stupid thing, like they <u>always</u> do, and they almost started swinging at each other. And there was my mother crying and my sister acting like it was no big deal, trying to make like she was the freaking United Nations or something, scrambling around trying to calm everybody down. Same old shit, different day. By the time dinner was done, I just wanted to throw up! I <u>hate</u> the holidays!" The longer she talked, the more hyper she got, and I watched her go from ice princess to wacky woman in about ten seconds flat. Finally, after she'd bled a lot of emotional blood, tears welled up in her eyes and she just stopped, stopped talking right in the middle of a sentence, and it was clear she was on the edge. It grew real quiet and I could feel the shared pain and support for Erica radiating from everybody else, including me. Suddenly, the silence was excruciatingly loud. Samantha, who was sitting next to Erica, slowly reached her long arm out and gently put her hand on Erica's shoulder, and Erica quietly started to sob.

After a short eternity, Susan spoke, saying, "It seems like this time of the year can be kind of hard for just about all of you," and most everybody nodded. She turned in my direction. "How about you, Molly? What do you think? How do you end up feeling this time of year?"

I had been sitting there feeling increasingly uncomfortable, not only because of the emotions spilling out around me but also because I knew the spotlight would shine on me sooner or later. And now, the lamp was lit. "I don't know," I said weakly. Everyone looked at me like they were waiting for something else.

"What do you mean, 'You don't know'?" Eric asked skeptically, and I had the distinct feeling he was speaking for the group.

"I mean I don't know," I answered defensively. "What do you want me to say?"

"We want you to not bullshit us," Harlan said, and I knew I must be on the spot because Harlan seemed like one of the more subdued kids in the group. Susan looked at him sharply with a be-careful look as no put-downs was a group rule. "What? Do you <u>buy</u> that bullshit?" He said to her. "<u>Everybody's</u> got an opinion about the holidays. We're supposed to tell the truth in here, aren't we? Well, all right, then, let's talk. Hey, look," he said while leaning out of his chair and gesturing with his hand extended, "I'm Jewish. Try <u>that</u> on for size in November and December in this town. I used to go home from school when I was little and cry. Can you believe that? I begged my parents to at least get a tree, so I could have <u>something</u> to brag about with all the Christian kids. When I'd go out on the street after the

25th and all the kids in my neighborhood would be zooming around with their new bikes, and showing off all their other loot, I just felt gypped. Then I'd ask my parents why Jewish kids didn't have Christmas or at least the kinds of presents they got. They'd talk to me some more about our religion and tried to build up Honika like it could compete with all the Christmas hoopla. When I got a little older I understood it better, but it still sucked to be left out of that whole damn parade, so don't talk to me about Christmas."

"So how would you say it made you feel?" Susan asked.

"Shitty!" Harlan said.

"Could you be a bit more specific, Harlan, and a little less graphic?" Susan asked, giving Harlan a small smile. "What kind of, uh, shitty? Mad shitty? Sad shitty? Hurt shitty? Confused?"

"Yes."

"Yes, what?"

"All of them. I felt all of them. Plus guilty. I felt guilty"

Confused, Joline piped up and asked, "Why did you feel guilty? I feel guilty after listening to you."

He looked her straight in the eyes. "Because," he said, "I'm Jewish, and for about two months every year I hated that."

There was a long silence after Harlan spoke, and Susan seemed to let the silence linger for a long time. Just when I thought I couldn't stand it anymore, Erica spoke. "I'm sorry, Harlan," was all she said.

"That's OK," he answered. "I'm used to it by now."

She looked at him like she was about to cry. "I'm sorry for that, too," she said.

Then, one by one, everyone offered an apology. It was "Sorry, dude," and "Hey, man, sorry," and "Harlan, I'm sorry, I never thought of it that way," and so on, until everybody had spoken. I was last. "Sorry," was all I said, and while I certainly felt it after listening, I didn't feel enough membership yet to say more.

"Thanks," he said collectively, and then the silence ruled again.

Susan let us twist in the wind for a while again, and then said, "I appreciate you sharing that with all of us. I've often thought it has to be difficult to be stuck in the middle of all the Christmas stuff in this country if you're of a different faith."

"It can be," he said. "It can be. It was for me."

Susan then just looked at me again. The room was getting smaller and smaller. "You were going to tell us something, Molly?"

"Oh, yeah." I cleared my throat. "I used to like them. The holidays, I mean."

"And you don't like them anymore?" Susan asked.

"Not especially."

"Why not?"

I squirmed a bit and said, "It's hard. You know, trying to pick out the right presents, making sure they're wrapped the right way, making sure everybody's happy. It's a lot of pressure."

Susan jumped right in and said, "Molly, you said something about making sure everybody's happy. I'm curious, why is that your job? Even more, if it is, how do you possibly do it? Make sure everybody's happy, that is." I heard an undercurrent of "Yeah," and "Right," and other heads nodded in agreement.

"It isn't easy," I said.

"I'll <u>bet</u> it's not," Susan said. "But, I'm still wondering how it ended up being your responsibility."

I had to stop and think for a minute, because I didn't want to sound as stupid as I suddenly felt. "Well, if I didn't, I'm not sure who would."

"What about your parents?" Eric asked. "Aren't they supposed to do it? Jeez, you make yourself sound like you're Santa Claus or something, and I don't see a big white beard or any reindeers." Most smiled and a few even snickered.

"I don't think I'm Santa Claus," I said defensively, and I was feeling increasingly cornered. "I just think it's important so I try to make sure I get my friends and family something nice. I don't have a lot of money or anything but I try to save a little bit or even try to make something if I can, but I'm not really good with my hands, like with the arts and crafts kind of stuff. I just know how much I look forward to it, or at least I used to, so I try to make sure others have a nice time, too. I don't think that's such a big deal. And I <u>don't</u> think I'm a saint, or anything."

"So, how does it go?" Philip asked.

"How does what go?" I asked, a bit confused.

"Your plans to make everybody happy."

I stopped and reflected on all the Ghosts of Christmas Past, and I sighed. "Pretty dang lousy, to tell you the truth."

"Why?" Philip asked. "What happened?"

"What happened? What didn't? Actually, let me take that back a bit. When I was little it was fun. But then, when I was a little older, the shit hit the fan between my parents. Oops," I said to Susan. "Sorry about the language."

Susan smiled and said, "Does anybody here have a problem with that?" They collectively shook their heads. "That's OK, Molly. Just keep going."

"Oh, OK, good. Anyway, after that, it got a bit hairy, and then they got divorced. And <u>then</u> it got really shitty." I looked at Susan and she just grinned. "After that, the ho-ho-ho was <u>definitely</u> gone, gone, gone. Anyway, I hate the holidays, too, just like everybody else here seems to."

"See," Sam said dramatically and loudly, "You're <u>not</u> alone," and everybody cracked up.

"Hey," Eric said, "Why don't we all sing some Christmas carols? Harlan, you game?"

"God knows I've heard them enough," Harlan said. "I'll tell you what. It's OK with me on one condition: I get to pick them!" Everybody yelled out in agreement all at once. "OK, then, let me hear a rousing chorus of 'Jingle Bells'. Better yet, let's do that in a round."

"What's a round?" Sam asked.

"The opposite of a square, you dope!" Justin called out, and everyone cracked up, this time including me.

"No, no," Harlan said, "that's when one person starts a song, then the next person picks it up a couple of words later, and then the next one, and so on. Didn't you ever do that in elementary school?"

Sam's light bulb went on, and she said, "Oh! I know, like doing row, row, row the boat," and she started singing it, "gently down the stream." As she finished, Justin took up the song, "Row, row, row the boat," and then Joline belted out, "Row, row, row the boat," and then, one by one, everyone was singing in a perfect round at the top of their voices, "Row, row, row the boat/ gently down the stream/ merrily, merrily, merrily, merrily/ life is but a dream." Harlan stood up on top of a chair and started directing, using a pencil Susan reached out and handed him, and then we all stood up, singing with our arms draped on each other's shoulders. I found myself singing to beat the band, and damn if we didn't sound good! After about fifteen reps or more, Harlan called out "One more time!" and we concluded with a rousing, inspirational flourish. When done, we all cracked up, and Philip proclaimed loudly, "If Christmas could be this much fun, I'd sign up to be the Santa at the Mall!" When we finally stopped laughing about ten minutes later, Susan said, "I think that's a wrap for today. Good group, Group!" For the first time in a long, long, time, I felt I belonged.

We walked back to our rooms, talking, laughing, and telling stories, some horrible, some not, about our childhood memories. In that one single hour, I learned something I never really knew before. I learned that shared pain is better than solitary pain, any day of the week. And I learned I could share it with others and survive. The world didn't come to an end. Actually, in some strange kind of way, it felt like the world began.

CHAPTER 10

It's weird. When you stay someplace you've never been before, it can feel really disorienting at first and you don't know your way around at all, like when you're on vacation somewhere and you wake up in the middle of the night with <u>no</u> clue where you are, how you got there, or how the hell to get to the bathroom. But then, after only a couple of days, you feel like you've always been there. You know all the secrets and tricks, like how to jiggle the toilet handle to get it to stop running, where the noises you hear in the middle of the night come from and when to expect them, and who to ask for what, and when, and how. I remember that feeling the few times we went camping when I was a little girl. I'd walk slowly and nervously to the camp playground, not knowing any of the kids on the swings. Then I'd awkwardly and sheepishly climb up the ladder to the sliding board after waiting nervously in line while all the other kids checked out the "new kid." But after only a day or two, I knew everybody's name, family, and campsite and I would adopt the same superior attitude I had endured with the next new kid who wandered onto the playground. It was the same thing here on the Unit. I'd been here only two days but I was already a "regular." Of course, this bonding process was probably accelerated by the fact that we had to pour our hearts out to each other every day, sharing our deepest, darkest secrets. Let's face it, once you've been seen stark naked, there ain't much more worth hiding, and God knows I had my fair share of turns walking around in my emotional birthday suit in the group sessions. I found that being exposed wasn't so bad once I overcame my initial embarrassment. It was a different story, however, when Susan told me my first family session was coming up that day.

"What's the matter?" she asked. "You don't look so good."

I just shrugged my shoulders.

"Look, Molly, I hope you know by now that it is <u>not</u> a good idea to keep the feelings inside. Tell me what you're thinking, <u>really</u> thinking. C'mon, fork it over!" She smiled.

"I'm just a little nervous. I haven't seen them since I got here, and I haven't had a conversation with both my mother and father like <u>together</u> in <u>ages</u>. I mean, c'mon, Susan! I'm gonna sit there with them and talk about what? The <u>family</u>? My feelings? <u>Their</u> feelings? Get real! The only damn thing they do is fight, and it doesn't matter who's there, or what I want, or what you want. All they do is fight." I realized I was getting a bit rude. "Sorry, I didn't mean to snap at you."

Susan cocked her head to the side. "You know, that's the first time I've heard you apologize for something since yesterday. You were on a real roll there for awhile." I smiled. "Molly, you'll survive. They'll survive. I won't kid you, it can be hard, and it can be emotional, for you and for them, but it can also be a chance for <u>all</u> of you to understand each other better, to get to <u>really</u> know each other. There can be family secrets that everybody carries around like thousand-pound weights hanging from their necks, and everyone tries to act like they're not there, but they are, Molly. They're there, and sometimes the only way to get rid of them is to talk about them. You look at theirs, and they look at yours, and together you might be able to help each other get the darn things off of each other. You guys can either drown by yourselves or swim together. There's not a lot of other choices, or at least no good ones."

"And you'll be there?"

"Yes, I will. I'm kind of the Master of Ceremonies. It's my job to make sure things go OK for all of you, because I know I'm asking all of you to stick your necks out. I referee the thing until you can all do that by yourselves. Because that's the <u>real</u> goal, Molly, for you guys to be able to do it when you need to after you leave. Does that make sense?"

I nodded.

"All right, then, good. You've got some time before your parents get here, so you can hang out until then."

As instructed, I did just that, hung out, lounging on my bed, watching TV, and otherwise wasting time, which <u>d-r-a-g-g-e-d</u> on by tick, by tock, and by tick. I made small talk with my peers, had a soda, stared at my hands, and otherwise made productive use of my time before Susan stuck her head inside my room. "OK, Molly, let's go. Your folks are here." I stood up, walked out the door, and followed her down the hall, and it strangely felt like I was going to meet them for the very first time, like they were complete strangers. Susan stopped in front of the same room where we went for Group. When I caught up to her, she smiled and gently put her hand on my shoulder. She gestured towards the room and I walked in with her following behind me.

I looked about as I walked in, and my mother and father were both there, sitting on two of the four chairs that had been set up. Strange, but suddenly the room looked completely different than it did when we had Group, and it was more than just the rearrangement of the chairs. It went from kind of big to sufficatingly small in a second. Both my parents looked over to me and smiled awkwardly as I entered, and Mom said brightly, "Hi, Molly, how are you?" with this hyper-animated expression.

"Fine, Mom," and I thought how we all just automatically barf that out when asked, even if it's far from true. Then again, what are the choices? Tell the truth? I don't think so. Nobody would talk to anybody if that were the case.

"Hi, honey," Dad said.

"Hi, Dad." They were both looking at me with these stupid smiles that said we're dying here, and I'm sure I had the same expression on my face because I was sure as hell squirming inside. Talk about tense!

"Have a seat, Molly," Susan said, and I weighed my chair choices, <u>carefully</u>. My parents were sitting next to each other, looking real unnatural while trying to look casual, and I chose the chair most directly opposite my mother rather than my father, and I felt self-conscious about the choice. I had to pick one of them, though. Suddenly, it felt like every decision could have symbolism, and I quickly resolved to be real cautious. Susan sat in the remaining chair. There was a silence of a couple of seconds that seemed like a couple of hours before Susan opened. "I want to thank all of you for coming because I know this isn't easy for any of you. As I explained, the purpose of this meeting is to give all of you a chance to talk to each other, but in a way I lied." We all looked at her a bit funny but she continued. "I lied because what I really want you to do even more than talk is to listen. Not just to hear, because I know you can all do that, but to <u>listen</u>. Many times, in our interactions with each other, we take a lot of stuff for granted, and believe we understand because we heard. But sometimes, what we might have heard might not be what the person speaking actually meant, or what that person really wanted us to hear. That can happen for a bunch of reasons, like being tired or distracted, or thinking about something that happened at work or at school, or the bills, or our friends, or something else. A lot of the time, actually most of time, we get lucky because what we're being told isn't that big a deal. Sometimes, though, it <u>is</u> a big deal, and that's when we need to listen. Obviously, there's stuff that's been a big deal for Molly, and we're here today to talk about that, OK?" Mom and Dad nodded. She explained the rules which were basically the same as they were for Group, and my parents nodded understanding. "All right, then. Who'd like to start? What do you all feel you need to talk about?"

The silence now was crushing, but I figured it sure as hell wasn't going to be me to open this puppy up. I was the kid, goddamit, and I wanted to be able to be the kid. Let them figure it out. Let them take the heat for awhile. I felt like I'd been taking it for a long, long time, and I was sick to death of it. While I may not have had much to say out loud, there was one heck of a lecture going on in my brain, but I was keeping it there. Susan was letting us all squirm but, unlike my parents, I'd grown used to it. Been there, done that. Here, I was the veteran and they were the rookies. Finally, Mom cracked. "I'd just like to know what led Molly to do this," she said, looking at Susan. "How she could feel so bad that she'd try to take her own life. I want to know what we did wrong. Most of all, I want to know what we can do to help her."

"Why don't you ask Molly?" Susan said.

"Oh, OK." Mom turned to me, looking at me with eyes that were both confused and nervous. "Why, Molly? Why? Why did you do it? What's so terrible that you felt you had to do this?" I wondered if we were all going to continue to refer to the dreaded event as the "this" or the "that." I suppose, however, that suicide attempts do create a bit of a categorization problem. "Suicide attempt" is a bit unwieldy, "killing yourself" is a tad crude, and "doing yourself in" is too vague, so I guess that the "this" or the "that" served a useful, albeit wimpy, purpose. Had to call it something.

"I don't know, Mom."

"You don't know? Do you have any idea how scared I was when I found you on the floor bleeding? How scared I am now?"

Susan interrupted. "Margaret, this is one of those times where I step in. Those are kind of what we call rhetorical questions, or questions that are either really kind of obvious or not possible to answer. It can put the receiver in a no-win situation. If you want Molly to know how scared you were, just tell her, OK?" Susan offered the advice in a gentle way with a smile on her face, but there was no mistaking what she meant. Again, I'd grown used to it, but now Mom and Dad were going through the learning curve. Mom had the look of someone at her first formal dinner trying to figure out which of the three forks to use for the salad.

"Oh, sorry."

I couldn't stifle the chuckle. "Now you sound like me, Mom."

"What?" she said. "What do you mean?"

"Never mind." Another day, maybe.

"So, Margaret, why don't you tell Molly?" Susan prompted.

"Tell her? Oh, yeah, that's right, I forgot." She grinned nervously, and started again. "We were really, really scared, Molly. When I found you with all that blood, with your blood, and it was everywhere. When I couldn't get you to wake up, and when I think of what could have happened...." but before she could finish the tears were welling up in her eyes and she was struggling, her lower lip quivering.

Susan rescued her. "Molly, what did your Mom say?"

I gave her a "duh" look. "That she was scared?"

"Are you asking or telling? And, by the way, tell your Mom, not me."

"Mom, you said you were scared."

"Yes, Molly, you can say that."

"What else did she say, Molly?" Susan didn't let anything go by.

"That she saw a lot of blood."

"And what else?"

"That she was worried about what could have happened."

"Is that about right, Margaret?"

Mom nodded.

"Good," Susan commented, "good." She then looked around at each of us. "I know some of this stuff sounds sort of simplistic and obvious, but when you get to the place where you guys are it's important to take real good care of the simplistic and the obvious, and to make sure misunderstandings don't creep in real sneaky-like, because I can <u>guarantee</u> that's happening with all of you. Words count. Gestures count. Even eye contact counts. And perhaps most importantly, listening counts. If you're careful with your messages and with their meaning, and careful with the impact they can have on the person who's on the receiving end, it helps keep the suckers from going haywire! And when you really hear what another person is saying, really wants you to hear, <u>then</u> you're having a conversation! Does that make sense?" Mom and Dad were listening intensely and nodding, and I think they were grateful for the guidance. Some lessons could only be learned through direct experience, though. "Molly, I think your Mom asked you another question before that last one. Something to the effect of what was bothering you before you cut your wrists?"

"Oh, yeah." I paused. Where should I begin here? Start with early childhood and move up, painful frame by painful frame, or fast forward right to adolescence? Quickly and succinctly summarize the divorce? Throw in a line or two about the years of silent sadness and terrible tension, and maybe a reference to the Bad Boy and sexual assault? Naw! "A whole lot of things, Mom. I can't just point to one thing."

"Well, then, can you point to something? Anything?" She looked at Susan. "Is that question OK?"

Susan smiled. "That's fine." Mom looked at me again.

"There's a <u>ton</u> of stuff that's been bothering me, Mom, a lot of stuff."

"Such as?"

"Like school...and home...and you guys. A lot of stuff, Mom! Which topic do you want to cover first?"

"I don't know, Molly. I guess the one that's the most important to you."

Susan said to my mom, "How do you feel things have been going in your family? What issues do you see that could be big problems for Molly, Margaret?"

Mom was quiet for awhile and glanced upwards, like the answer might come from on high. Moments passed, inspiration must have been found, and she sighed a bit and began. "I know it hasn't been easy for either Molly or Josh since we split up, but I think she's had a pretty good life." She turned to me. "After all, it's been how many years? I just assumed you were over it by now. If you weren't, I sure couldn't tell."

I glared at her, and Susan noticed. "Can you respond to that, Molly? What did hear your mom say?"

My heart was beating faster and faster. "That's the problem, Mom. That's the problem. You didn't know because you didn't <u>want</u> to know!"

"Molly, I asked you to summarize what your mom said."

"All right, all right! You said you thought I should have been fine, that my life was fine."

"What I heard, Molly, was your mom saying it's been hard for you and your brother but she feels it's been a good life and she thought you'd be over it by now. Is that about it, Margaret? Am I on target?"

"Yes, that's pretty accurate."

"OK, Molly, try it again."

"You said it's been hard for me and Josh but you think I should be over it now." I looked at Susan, realizing that the contemptuous tone in my voice was probably glaringly obvious. "OK?" She looked at Mom who nodded.

"All right, Molly, good. Now, you were telling your mom and dad what you thought before I interrupted. Why don't you tell them again. How you feel now, how you felt then. If you agree or disagree with what your mom said."

As I sat there, it occurred to me that this was a landmark first. I'd never been asked that before by my parents. Never! Oh, sure, we talked about it, but it was much more about being talked to rather than with, at least in regard to the divorce. Such as, you know, "We'll make it up to you," (yeah, right), and "You'll get over it," (I don't think so!). I also wondered, why not? Why wasn't I asked? Asked what I thought, and how I felt. So, I figured I'd just say that. It kinda felt like jumping off the diving board for the first time but this time I wasn't at all sure how hard the water was. But, you're never going to swim if you don't stick your toes in the water.

"Why didn't you ask me, Mom? Huh? Why didn't you ask me, Dad? Huh? How come neither of you ever asked me how I was? How would you know how I was doing? You never asked! Never! You just wanted to believe I was fine because you couldn't deal with me not being fine. Both of you were so busy fighting with each other that you didn't have the time to wonder or care about how me and Josh were feeling. Shit, Mom, you spent almost all your time in your bedroom crying and Dad, you spent almost all your time at work, or golfing, or wherever the hell you were! I don't know where it was, but it sure wasn't with us. So, how's that? Huh? If you want to know what some of my problems are, just take a look in the mirror!" I was having a hard time getting the words out right, as my breathing was all screwed up (same old, same old) and my voice was kinda squeaky and high. I was inhaling when I should have been exhaling, and exhaling when I should have been inhaling. I was excited in a real nervous kind of way, and in one burst I'd said stuff I'd never had the nerve to say before. My right leg was bouncing furiously up and down. The water was deep and hot, damn hot! And I was in way over my head. But, I had my lifeguard, Susan, sitting there so I felt I could keep my head up, at least for now, but I was treading water like crazy.

There was an extended period of silence after my speech, and Susan seemed to let it just hang in the air for awhile while I regrouped. My parents' eyes were wide and round, and my mom's lower lip was quivering. Dad just looked uncomfortable and cleared his throat about a hundred times and I was busy trying not to hyperventilate again. Eventually, Susan spoke. "Thanks, Molly. I know that wasn't easy." I knew I had broken just about all of her group rules, but for some reason she didn't point out my boo-boos, probably just out of sympathy. "Steve, that was a lot, but what did you hear Molly say there? How would you summarize what she said?"

Dad got in another throat clearing and shifted in his chair. He waved his hands symmetrically, like some kind of new sign-language, before speaking. "Well, Susan.." and Susan jumped in.

"Tell Molly, Steven."

"Oh, right. Well, Molly, what I think you said is that, uh, it's been hard for you and we, uh, never asked you how you were feeling, or how things affected you."

"Anything else, Steven?"

Dad crossed his legs and then uncrossed them. "You, uh, said something to the effect that you felt we weren't there for you, Molly."

"Molly, how about it? Is that about what you said, what you wanted to be heard?"

"More or less." Susan looked at me closely like she was weighing whether to let that go by without editorial comment and must have decided it was close enough.

"What would you want to say in response to that? Steven? Margaret? Do you agree with Molly? Do you think she has a point?"

My dad spoke first. "I don't know where to start, Susan, which point to respond to first," and he had a pained look and pleading tone that begged for understanding.

"How about Molly's belief that you didn't want to know how she felt, or at least avoided asking how she felt? Why don't we start there?"

My parents looked at each other with facial expressions asking who'd go first and, much to my suprise, Dad opened. "Uh, you're probably right, Molly, we might have overlooked your opinions to some extent when we were separating, but you need to understand, it was a very hard time for us. We didn't want to drag you into our problems, and we thought we were doing the right thing by shielding you and Josh from our problems as much as we could."

"Do you really think you were 'shielding' us, Dad? Do you really believe we didn't know what was going on? What did you think we were? Blind? Deaf? <u>Dumb</u>? They were our problems, too, Dad. It was our life, too!"

Susan intervened. "Molly, please, first summarize what your Dad said. And remember, tell him, not me."

I sighed, rolled my eyes, and looked at my father. "You said I was right. No, wait, you said I was <u>probably</u> right about you guys not paying attention to us, and you were trying to keep us out of your problems. You said <u>we</u> needed to understand you."

Susan looked to my father for his reaction, and he sort of shook his head from side to side like adults do when they're disappointed in a kid's naiveté. He cocked his head from one side to the other. "I didn't quite mean it that way."

"Yes, you did," I snapped. "That's <u>exactly</u> what you meant!"

"Hold on, Molly, hold on," Susan said. "Steven, you want to clarify what you said?"

"OK, maybe that's what I said, but it's not what I meant."

Again, Susan asked, "What <u>did</u> you mean, Steven?"

"Oh, I don't know how to explain it the right way. It was a long time ago. Things were pretty crazy then. Heck, we were pretty crazy. We wanted to do the right thing by you kids but we didn't know what the right thing was, or how to do it. We <u>honestly</u> thought it was better to not talk about it too much. We were a lot younger then, too, Molly, and we probably made mistakes." I glared at him.

Susan looked at me. "Molly?"

"You're saying you're sorry?"

"I think so. I'm trying."

"Well, then, can I ask you something, Dad?"

"Sure."

"Where've you been?"

He looked a little puzzled. "You know where I've been, Molly, I've been in...."

"No, Dad, I mean, <u>where</u> have you been? All these years. <u>All</u> these years. You don't know me! You don't know me <u>at all</u>. Heck, there's been times I think I could have waltzed right in front of you on the street and you wouldn't have even recognized me. You could've run me over and you wouldn't have known me. What did you think, Dad? Huh? That when you divorced Mom that you divorced us? <u>Where</u> have <u>you</u> <u>been</u>, Dad?"

"Now, wait a minute, Molly! Wait a minute! I've provided for both you and your brother since the divorce. Do you know how much I've paid in support since I left? How hard it is for me to pay the child support and then support my own home? I think I deserve <u>some</u> credit for what <u>I've</u> had to sacrifice."

"Steven," Susan said somewhat forcefully.

"What?"

"Please. What did Molly tell you?"

Dad let some air out forcefully through his nose, almost snorting. He looked at me with an intensity I hadn't seen in years, but sure recalled instantly. "You said I don't know you anymore."

"No, Dad. I'm saying you <u>never</u> did."

"Now it's my turn?" he asked Susan, who nodded. "Then let me tell you something, Molly. Maybe I haven't been there for you the way I should have been. I'll admit that. But all this time I've had to try to divide myself between the family I had and the family I have. I can't be in two places at the same time. I can divide myself only so far. But I have worked darn hard to provide for two families, and I have paid every penny I'm supposed to pay, Molly. Every penny! I should get some credit for that. Some respect."

Before Susan cued me, I responded. "You're saying I should realize how hard it's been for you. That you deserve credit. You deserve respect."

"Darn right! Is that too much to ask?"

I looked at Susan. "Can I answer him now?" She nodded. "Well, Daddy, in my opinion, I feel that's about typical for you. You know? Real typical. It's about the money, and it's about you. But let me tell <u>you</u> something, Daddy. I wish, you don't know how <u>much</u> I wish, I could give you back every penny, <u>every</u> <u>single</u> <u>penny</u>. Maybe then you could take <u>all</u> <u>that</u> <u>money</u> and buy yourself a clue about me, about what it means to be a father, <u>my</u> father, and about how I feel every damn day! We're not your kids, Dad. C'mon, be honest. For once, be honest. Let's face it, we were a mistake. We're the 'problem' from your previous life, the financial 'problem' you're stuck with, and I think you believe you can just excuse yourself from it with a check! Well, we're a lot more than that, Dad. So, here it is, Daddy. You ready? Do you want to know the <u>big</u> secret? What I needed, Daddy, was a <u>father</u>. A father!" I started to cry. "I needed <u>you</u>, Daddy, not your lousy money. I needed you. I needed you! And you weren't there." Now I was sobbing. "So keep your money, Daddy. OK? Just keep it. I don't want it. I don't want it."

My mom suddenly spoke up. "Molly, you shouldn't be so hard on your father. It wasn't all his fault."

You've got to realize that the intense emotions I had and the words coming out of my mouth almost had a mind of their own. It was like someone else was thinking the thoughts and then speaking them, but I knew it was more a sudden awakening, a revelation, a recognition of feelings that had been swallowed and subdued for so many years. Now that this gate had been opened, there was no holding back the stuff spilling out. "You know, Mom, you're absolutely right," I said. "You're absolutely right. It hasn't just been Dad, it's been you, too."

She had this shocked look on her face. "Me?"

"Yes, you!"

"What, Molly? What did I do?"

"What did you do? What did you do? Mom, do you have any idea how many times I've had to comfort you? How many times I've been the one telling you that things would be OK? How many times I've watched you cry, and ended up felt shitty about it? Do you, Mom?"

"Molly, you don't understand, I never intended to..."

"Oh, please, Mom, don't start with that! Don't tell me how I misunderstood you. Don't tell me about what you meant to do or didn't mean to do. It's always been about your pain, and your sadness, and your hard times. You want everyone to know just how much you've been hurt, and how life has cheated you. Well, who do you think has been on the receiving end of those messages most of the time, Mom? Yeah, it's been me and Josh. Try to picture what it's been like to be me, Mom, to be there while you dissed Dad over and over and over. I got so sick of it!"

Mom just sat there with this sad, shocked look on her face, her mouth half open. Ordinarily, I would have felt bad, would have felt responsible, would have scrambled to make her feel better. Today, I just felt anger. She started to cry.

"Oh, that's great, Mom. That's <u>so</u> typical. When the going gets tough, you cry. You are the <u>queen</u> at feeling bad for yourself, and guess what, Mom? Guess who's been left to deal with that, Mom? Who was left to try to make you feel better? Yeah, me, that's who! I wasn't supposed to be your support, Mom, you were supposed to be mine. I was just a little girl, Mom, a little girl! I wasn't your buddy, or your counselor, or your shrink. I was your daughter. Whatever has been terrible in your life has been terrible in mine, and <u>none</u> of it was my fault, Mom. None of it!"

"Margaret?" Susan said.

Mom was frozen, her face fixed in a strange stare that was pointed in my direction but somehow not there. It was hard to tell if she was breathing or not.

"Margaret?" Susan said again.

Mom moved a bit, but her stare stayed in place. She made this half-sigh, half-snort sound, like she had been punched in the stomach. "I don't....I don't," and she paused. "I don't know what to say. I never... I didn't know you felt that way. I never meant to hurt you. I didn't realize you hated me so much."

"Damn it, Mom, you're doing it again! This isn't about you! This about me! Me, Mom. Remember me? And if you think I hate you, then you <u>really</u> don't get it."

"I'm so sorry, Molly," Mom said with a cracking voice. "I'm so sorry. I'm so sorry. I didn't realize how you were hurting. I didn't realize how I hurt you. I'm so sorry."

I was drained. I was shaking. I couldn't breathe right. Mom was crying softly. Suddenly, I was overwhelmed at this scene, at the emotion, and I started to cry. Susan reached out and touched my arm, and I hung my head as I cried. At one point, though, in between the sobs, I thought I heard something strange, something odd, and I instinctively looked up and through my tear-clouded eyes, I saw something remarkable. There sat my father, and he, too, was crying. Through it all, the family pain, the arguments, the separation, the divorce, and the years of heartache since, I had never seen him cry, not once. And now there he was, right in front of me, his face pressed tightly in his hands, and he was letting out a sound that made me think of a wailing wild animal. In between the wails he was sucking air big-time in hard, staccato gasps that punctuated his crying like a series of emotional exclamation marks. There's something that's pitiful and unnerving about seeing a grown-man cry, probably because you generally never see or hear it, but to watch your father fall apart is an particularly bizarre reversal of position, especially a father from who I was fundamentally estranged. To add to the Twilight Zone effect, my mother had her hand gently resting on his shoulder, and she was quietly crying, too. It was all <u>way</u> too weird, a sardonic family bonding session, and it made me cry even more. It was like we were all mourning the loss of family faith and innocence those many years ago, and we finally found something we had in common, something we all shared. Pain.

We continued with the tears and Susan let us go on, and the quiet sounds of sobs floated in the air like a strange sad choir. Ironically, it was the first thing we had shared together as a family in years and years. After a while, we started to regain control, gradually slowing first to sniffles and then to sighs. Eventually, we were all left with that drained emotional hangover you get after such a dramatic and highly personal confrontation. Spent. Exhausted. Numb. Stunned.

Finally, Susan spoke. "Thanks, all of you. Thank you. I know that wasn't easy. But it was important. It was a good piece of work. I think some things that needed saying were said. And I think some things that needed to be heard were heard. Are you all OK?" One by one, we nodded, and we anxiously looked at each other as if to gauge the sustained damages. Something big had happened, and we all knew it. I had seen Mom in such a state many times over the years, and the look of loss on her face was all too familiar to me. However, it was my first experience with Dad letting it all hang out, and he had an expression that was a mixture of puzzlement and hurt. He looked confused. His face was red and blotchy, and the light reflected off the tracks of the tears on his cheeks. And God help me, I felt sorry for him, and nobody could have been more surprised by that than I was.

"I think it should be clear to you at this point that there's much to be discussed among you," she said, "and that it's not a walk in the park to discuss it. I hope, though, that it's also clear that you've <u>got</u> to. Molly, I know that the hurt that led you to hurt yourself lies in the stuff that exists among <u>all</u> of you," and she included each of us with a broad sweep of her arm around the room. Then, looking directly at my parents, she said, "It also seems to me that the both of you have your own ghosts that you need to exorcise. Margaret, you're Molly's mom, the only one she'll ever have. And Steven, you're Molly's dad, the only one she'll ever have. Those rolls don't have to be mutually exclusive, even if you are divorced."

My father looked at her, and his eyes were pleading. "Can you help us do that, Susan? Is it too late? Can you help us?"

"I'll do everything I can, Steven."

My mom then joined my father's gaze. "We'll do everything we can, too, Susan." She then turned to me. "We will, Molly. We will."

I was blown away by the emotional winds that had blown into the room during the past hour, my head hurt, and my eyes were about ready to explode. I'd heard things I'd never heard before, and never thought I'd hear. Part of me felt some faint rumblings of hope, and part of me thought I should run like crazy and hide under the nearest table for protection. Sure, it's great to come and say the right thing when you're under the heavy pressure of the therapy thumb, but it's another thing to follow through when it's just another manic Monday, and the lunch meat is all bad, and the last check bounced, and the support payment is overdue, and it's raining or snowing or sleeting or some damn thing for the umpteenth day in a row, and everybody in the world wishes they were someone else that day. It's another thing when you go back home to your trophy bride and the second-chance kids and the alter-ego you adopted after you stepped out of the divorce phone-booth in your "I'm Reborn" uniform, complete with long flowing cape blowing in the wind, just like freakin' Super Man. But, skepticism not withstanding, it went better than I had hoped for. They looked like they just possibly cared, and I think deep down that's what I really wanted. Maybe they can even come to understand. And maybe, just maybe, I could, too. "I hope so, Mom," I said. "I hope so."

Susan wrapped up the session with some summaries of the issues raised and the points made, but I doubt any of us heard much of what she said, as we were all pretty rung out. I did hear her say that this was a good beginning but it was just that, a beginning. There was much more work to be done and none of us disagreed. Mom and Dad said good-bye to me, and each gave me a hug. When Dad reached out to me with his arms, we both looked at each other with polite caution and trepidation but we took a chance. We hugged. It was the first hug between us since I turned thirteen, and there wasn't exactly a ton of hugs prior to that, so this was bizarre to the max. However, strange as it might sound, it felt incredibly intense, and meaningful, and important. He squeezed me tight, and he rocked ever so slightly from side to side, and I hugged him back. "I'm sorry, Molly," he whispered softly in my ear. "I'm so sorry."

"I am, too, Daddy. I am, too," and I meant that in all ways possible. Finally, he released me, and Susan made some closing comments designed to bring the powwow to an end. She led my parents out the door and down the hall as I followed. At the door, they said good-bye, turned and left. As the door slowly closed, I watched them walk down the hall and I wondered what their small talk would be on the way out to their respective cars. I wondered if they'd just return to their usual Cold War positions, or would they actually compare their Mom-and-Dad notes? Would they take up the skirmish in the absence of Susan's referee whistle, or would they actually talk to each other, and listen to each other, and hope and plan together for me? For Josh? Talk about a long shot. Suddenly, I was trying to remember what I had read once about the odds on winning the Lottery. But, like they say in the commercials, you can't win if you don't play. So, we'll see. We'll see. Everybody loves a long shot.

CHAPTER 11

I've got to tell you, this whole experience opened my eyes to a number of things I had never seen or considered before, but perhaps the biggest revelation was that a family is in many ways a living, breathing animal that is born, and grows, and learns, and hurts, and needs, and bleeds, and if ignored and neglected, dies. Also, like all living things, a family is like a collection of interrelated organs, and while each organ is critical and important in its own right, it's useless if not connected to the others. Each needs the other in order to survive. I also figured out that "family" is a relative term, and that some are made by circumstances and are temporary, like the kids who became a precious family in abscentia for me in the hospital, and others are made by birth and are static, like the Mom and the Dad and the Brother and the Sister. We have different versions of family at many different levels, with many different meanings.

My hospital family became very special to me, even though its members changed on a frequent basis, because my "siblings" and I spent our days bonding, whether we wanted to or not. Thankfully, my natural family hung tight with me, too, and Mom <u>and</u> Dad made it to every session, and even Josh came to some of the sessions when appropriate, as he was hurting in his own way, too. I don't know if I changed because of them, or if they mutated first which in turn led to my change. See? A living, breathing animal. I remember my biology teacher saying that "the whole is greater than the sum of the parts," and I had no damn idea what he really meant by that. Now, I did. What I also knew is that I started to not feel alone, and I started to not feel lonely. It wasn't an "Aha!" experience with some sudden cosmic vision of the truth. Rather, it was a gradual transformation where some period of time would pass and

I'd realize I hadn't felt bad. That's not to say that there weren't times when I was stressed, because I think part of the plan is to expose you to it and see how you handle it. After some time, though, I found myself just recognizing what was bugging me and saying it, first to myself and then directing it to the person or the problem that caused it, and not to myself. After the last session with my family, Susan was talking to me about the issues that were raised and how I felt about them. You know, like she always did. While we were talking, she asked in a casual, offhand way, "By the way, Molly, how long has it been since you've felt like cutting?" She caught me by surprise because I realized I hadn't even thought about it for awhile.

"Now that you mention it, Susan, it didn't even cross my mind."

She smiled. "Good. <u>Good</u>! Now, please keep that in mind after you leave here and you hit the wall. And Molly, you <u>will</u> hit the wall. We all do. But the stuff here has worked because you learned that you need to do the work, and you learned how to do the work."

"Hey," I said, "You helped me."

"I just helped you use the ability you already had in yourself that kinda got lost under some pretty big piles of stuff. It wasn't magic, Molly, and it wasn't me. It was you, and you did the work. And you can do the work again, when you need to, and it can work again. Don't forget that, OK? <u>Please</u>, don't forget that! You <u>always</u> have another choice. OK?"

"OK."

"<u>Really</u>?" she asked with an exaggerated, comical whine in her voice.

"Yes, <u>really</u>!" I answered, whining even louder, and then laughing.

"Shake on it?" Susan asked, extending her hand.

"Sure," I answered, "It's a deal." She grasped my hand with both of hers, and squeezed tightly. I looked at her and she was gazing at me with her big brown eyes that blazed with an intensity I hadn't seen before. She smiled and I smiled back, and suddenly I found myself reaching over to her and hugging her with all my might. She hugged back, and we sort of rocked back and forth for awhile. "Thank you, Susan," I said. "Thank you. I'll never forget you."

"I won't forget you either, Molly. And you're welcome." There was a closure that took place at that very moment, and I realized I was better. Not cured, mind you, but better, like after you've had barfalonus for a day or so, sick as can be, scared to put even water in your stomach, but eventually start to feel a bit hungry and think you can handle some toast. That kind of better. After awhile, we mutually loosened our grips. Susan patted me warmly on my shoulders before letting go. "I was going to tell you this tomorrow, but the moment seems right now. I've discussed your progress with the Team, and we all feel you're about ready, Molly. I think you know it, too."

"You mean to go home? Like for good?"

"Yes, Molly. Home. For good. Hopefully! That's the plan." Susan was right, as usual. I think I had that feeling for awhile but, like most things with me, it had been more of a feeling than a thought. Now that she had put it into words, though, I knew she was right. Lately, when looking out the Clinic windows, I found myself wondering about life "out there," and I was able to actually visualize myself back at school, and back at home. I had no real idea how I was going to handle the transition, but that concern was offset by the gnawing feeling that I should be there. Part of me was scared to death, but part of me was also a bit excited, and a bit itchy. I also had wondered about Craig. A lot. Even though we were only just getting to know each other, I missed him, and hoped he missed me, at least a little bit. But, c'mon, how long could I expect him to wait around, especially for the likes of me?

"So, when does it happen? How does it happen? Did you talk to my parents about it? Are they ready for it?" I was getting hyper.

"Calm down, Molly!" Susan said, smiling. "Calm down. We'll work out the particulars in a day or so. There's what's called a Discharge Plan that we'll put together with you and your parents that specifies what we believe is important for you to keep up your progress back home, and together we'll set goals, make plans for those goals, set up your therapy for when you get home, and other stuff like that, but you don't need to worry about that right now. So, how does that all sound to you? You OK with that?"

"Yeah, Susan, I'm OK with that." And I was.

"Great! I'll give you more details as they come up. Any questions?"

I just shook my head.

"OK, if you get any, just ask."

"I will, I promise."

She smiled and left. I sat on the edge of my bed and looked around the room, at the Holiday Inn quality picture of flowers that hung on the wall, at the heap of clothes, magazines, and other clutter piled high on Sam's bed, and the dressers, mirrors, and closet that we shared. Up to now, I hadn't really considered the fact that all of this was only a temporary refuge, and I think I had either relaxed with the notion of this place as "home" or, more likely, just avoided acknowledging the inevitable. Now, however, here it was. One of those classic "win-lose" situations. Yeah, I was scared. No, let me correct that. I was <u>petrified</u>! But I was ready.

As I was deep into my reflections on all this, Sam strolled in and bellowed, "Hey, girl, what's up?"

I swear, Sam was the perkiest depressed girl I ever knew. I realized that this was the beginning of the end of our relationship too, and that made me sad. We had grown to be more than just friends, and had shared experiences over a short period of time that I imagine most people don't share over a lifetime. Sam knew me, and I knew her. On the surface, Sam looked like she had it together, and she spent a lot of her time "counseling" everybody else, including me. Underneath the louder than necessary voice and the outrageous comments, however, she was as fragile as those delicate animals in that play, <u>The Glass Menagerie</u>. Sam had nicks and chips and dings all over her, but you had to really know her to see them, and I had. Late at night, when everybody else was sleeping, I could often hear her quietly crying in her bed, but I'd usually pretend to be asleep because I knew she hated to be caught with her guard down, looking vulnerable. She found the whole thing <u>so</u> embarrassing. I knew she wasn't going to be leaving any time real soon, and I suddenly felt guilty that it looked like I would be. When I first came, she looked like she had it relatively together, at least compared to me. However, I could see that over time I had changed, and Sam had stayed the same. It's not that she was any worse, she just didn't seem any better. I had the feeling that Sam was going to be at this for awhile, and she had even told me recently that there was some talk about her being moved to a more long-term care kind of place. I tried to figure out how to tell her what I had just been told, couldn't think of anything snappy, so decided to just let it out.

"Susan just told me that I'm probably going home soon."

Samantha got one of those expressions that says "I'm confused about how I really feel about this" but recovered pretty quick. "Hey, that's great! I'm glad one of us is getting sprung from the slammer. When are you getting out?"

"I'm not really sure. Susan said something about making a Discharge Plan or some damn thing, but she wasn't real clear about when."

"Oh, yeah, I've heard about those Discharge thingies, and I think I even got close to one myself at one point, but you know how that goes. But, hey, you girl, you're going to do it! You're going to do it!"

"It looks like it. I think so."

"I <u>know</u> so, Molly. I know so."

Sam trotted over to me and reached down with her long arms, wrapping them around me. I seemed to be doing a lot of hugging today. She squeezed me tight, and I don't think she knew her own strength because she was crushing me, but that was OK. She patted me on the back like I was a baby, and I hugged her back but I was no match for her. Sam was the sister I never had, and I was losing her. I wondered why all gain had to come with some degree of loss and why happiness could never be absolute. I think I then understood what the term "bittersweet" meant. She broke the clinch and looked at me, and she was crying.

"Hey, don't cry. It's all right."

"What are you talking about?" she asked. "You're crying, too," and darned if I wasn't, the tears rolling in waves down my cheeks. There we were, both of us bawling, looking absolutely pitiful. Suddenly, we both let out a high-pitched wail at the same time that <u>really</u> sounded ridiculous and we then both broke out laughing at the dramatic comedy roles we were playing. We laughed and laughed, and I was holding my sides with the ache you get from laughing too loud and long. It was good, though, real good, and we moved past the pain. It was like a closing ceremony of sorts, and we pledged to keep in touch and stay close, but down deep I think we both knew that wasn't likely to happen. It was easier to have the illusion, though, because sometimes the truth is too cruel. What one needs to do is find a way to put a veil over it so it's not so glaring. That way, you know it's there but it doesn't sting as much. We talked some more about what I was going to do when I went home, and Sam talked about her hopes and plans back in the real world, and neither of us found it necessary to weight the rationality of those plans. Why ruin a perfectly good fantasy? We then went out to the Commons area and Sam let everybody else in on the news after asking me if it was OK. Heck, that was just <u>fine</u> with me, it saved me the trouble. There was more hugging, and congratulations, and "Let's stay in touch" from my colleagues. I felt like a minor celebrity. Some of the people I'd really miss, and others not so much, but overall the whole trip had been more positive than not.

The next day, in Group, Susan formally made the announcement that I'd be leaving the next day, and everyone again said good-bye in their own ways. Susan always used the successful departure of any of us as an opportunity to point out what the graduate had done to reach this point, and she stressed the progress she felt I had made in being able to recognize the feelings that I used to hide inside and how I had learned to put pain into words, and to actually share it with others, and to move past it. It felt nice to be bragged about, and I remembered how I had looked up to the "veterans" when I had first arrived. Now, it was me.

Susan had also asked me if she could talk about my cutting at this session, as she felt that sharing my experiences might be of help to the others, as cutting wasn't exactly an isolated occurrence in this place, and I had told her OK.

"As some of you know," she said, "Molly has also struggled with the problem of self-mutilation, which is a fancy term for hurting one's self, and in her case it was about cutting herself, and I know some of the rest of you wrestle with that problem, too. Molly, what do you think got you started with cutting?"

While I had certainly shared a lot about my problems while here, I never really felt like I was any kind of an "example" for anyone else, but now here I was with everyone else looking at me, waiting for me to inform them.

I cleared my throat a bit and began. "Actually, I'm not sure where to begin. It's a bit strange to feel like I'm in a position to 'help' any of you, because you guys have all helped me so much. It's even weirder to think that telling you about my problems with cutting could possibly give anybody else the strength to resist it, but as I thought about it when Susan asked me, I wondered what it might have been like for me if somebody else had told me about it." I paused and cleared my throat again, and instinctively said "Sorry." But then, to my surprise, I said "No, wait a minute. I'm <u>not</u> sorry. It's pretty normal to do that, and you all have also helped me to learn that I've got to let myself off the hook easier. So, I'm not going to apologize. You see, that was part of my problem, too. I felt like I was at least partly responsible for either causing everybody else's problems or being a loser because I couldn't help them with the ones they had, and now I know it's enough work to try to handle my own. I can help, but I can't take the blame. So, I'm <u>not</u> sorry! Deal with it!" Everyone chuckled.

"So, where was I? Oh, yeah, the cutting! You know, I had heard some girls talk about it here and there, there were rumors and stuff, and I also saw something about it on some news show on TV once, but I never paid much attention to all that stuff, because I didn't think it had anything to do with me. Little did I know, huh? Well, things got really heavy all over the place, which most of you know about, and I couldn't take it any more. The pressure was like, you know, too much. I felt like I was going to <u>explode</u>! I didn't know what to do, or who to tell, and even if I did, I thought nobody would want to hear about my pitiful problems. So, one night, when I was really feeling like crap, I took the top from my BIC pen and scratched my arm with it. You know, with a scratch that looks like one you get when catch yourself on a sharp edge or something. I felt <u>really</u> stupid, but I also felt like I was able to distract myself or something, like I moved the pain from my head to my arm. After that, it wasn't long before I was using sharper and sharper stuff to cut, and then I wasn't satisfied until I saw blood. It kind of became my 'drug,' and I was a junkie, big time."

There was this kid, Luke, who made this face when I said that and then made this noise that said "yeah, <u>right</u>!" I looked at him. "What?" he said.

"You don't believe me, Luke?"

"Well, c'mon, isn't that a bit of an exaggeration? I mean, cutting yourself is like a drug? I gotta be honest with you, I've done my share of them, of drugs, that is, and I have a hard time believing that cutting is a fun way to get high! I've got <u>lots</u> better ways," and everyone chuckled a bit.

"Luke..." Susan started to say, and I interrupted her.

"No, that's OK, Susan," I said. "That's OK." I turned to Luke again. "I know it sounds crazy, and after awhile you start to feel really crazy, because you know it's just plain nuts to be making yourself bleed and to be hiding stuff around the house to slash yourself with. I don't really understand it myself. But, I'm not bullshiting you guys.

That's what happened with me. I can't tell you why anybody else does it, I can only tell you about me. I'm <u>not</u> lying!"

I think I got Luke's attention. "All right, man, all right! I believe you, OK? Don't rip my lungs out!"

"I wouldn't lie to you about this. Really! I don't want anybody else to go through what I've been through. You don't want to go through this. By the time I got here, I was so disgusted with myself, I couldn't stand it. I'd look at myself in the mirror and want to throw up. I felt like I was the lowest, slimiest, most worthless excuse for a human walking the face of the earth. And I'll tell you, that's not something you go around bragging about. I mean, who are you going to tell? All your 'buds?' I couldn't tell them, and I also really believed nobody would give a damn if I did. Who could possibly care about me? That's what I thought. And the cutting was like the world's biggest distraction from that I could think of, and I also felt somehow like I deserved it, like I deserved to bleed. I felt like it kinda served me right for being such a useless piece of shit, such a loser."

Everybody was looking at me with these wide eyes, but there was a lot of feeling there, too, because for the large part we grew to care about each other. "How do yo feel now?" Susan asked.

"Different. I'm not sure if that means better, and I want to be careful before I go around bragging about anything in case I might jinx myself, but I think it is. Better, I mean."

Susan pressed, "How is it different for you?"

I smiled, and said, "You have a real knack for the tough questions, Susan," and everyone laughed, with a spattering of comments like "You got <u>that</u> right!"

"It's a tough job," Susan joked, "but <u>somebody's</u> got to do it."

"And I'm so glad you do," I answered, without even thinking about it. Again, there was a mixed chorus of approving responses, and even a bit of clapping, all of which made Susan blush, and that was real cute. "How I think it's different for me now is that I feel like I have a bunch of things I can do when I get stressed instead of cutting. I can tell somebody, and not just assume that no one cares. All of you guys are a good example of that. I can write about it, and I've found that helps a lot. You know, take the feelings out and put them on paper, and then I can look at them, and there kind of outside me, at least a little bit. I can do my relaxation, to take an edge off the crappy feelings. Or I can just wait a while, wait for the feelings to go down a little bit, and not just act on it when they first creep into my brain. You know, stuff like that. Obviously, I haven't been on the outside yet to try this in real life, but I feel confident, really confident, and that's a real miracle all by itself."

Charlene, this new kid, asked, "Didn't it hurt?"

"Yeah, it hurt. That was the whole point."

She had this confused look. "That's really weird," she said. "I don't get it."

Then, to my surprise, this boy Carl, who was there for depression kinds of stuff but had never said much about this stuff in Group, spoke up. "Hey," he said to Charlene, "pain comes in different ways. You never know when it might jump up and bite you on the butt. At least Molly was able to kind of control it with the cutting. She could decide when it was going to happen, and how much it was going to happen. It's all about control, man, it's all about control."

"Good point, Carl," Susan said. "Molly, do you think you need that kind of pain, that kind of control anymore?"

"No, Susan, I don't. What I think is I feel like I've got hope, and the answer's all about hope. I also feel like I've got a lot more control than I used to have, at least over myself, and what I think and feel. The cutting never solved a darn thing, it just hurt my body. And, boy, can it look gross!"

That was pretty much the end, and Susan wrapped things up. I spent the rest of the night hugging, getting hugged, etc., and Sam and I stayed up late giggling, making predictions about our futures, and guessing and making bets on how everybody else would make out, and so on. Sam fell asleep first, snoring like she always did, and I eventually drifted off on that last night on the "inside." I dreamed about stuff that was fairly pointless and harmless, like your typical run-of-the-mill dream, and I figured that was a good omen. No demons. Not a single one.

CHAPTER 12

I was up early the next day, but I had slept well. Obviously, I was wound up and excited, and more than a little nervous about going home, even though I had only been at the Clinic for ten days. In some ways, it seemed like it was much longer than that and, in others, it seemed like I had just got there. Space travel is deceiving. I did breakfast with Sam and everybody else with butterflies in my stomach, and finished packing the stuff I had, even though it was pretty much ready to go. I just kind of pushed it around and played with it to pass the time. Everybody else was going about the day as usual, and it felt odd to not be part of it. Even Sam left to join the day's activities, giving me one last bear-hug, and there I was, waiting. Discharge time was 10:00 in the morning, and Susan stayed with me most of the time as the seconds ticked off like hours. Eventually, she popped in. "Time to go, Molly, your parents are here."

I jumped up and grabbed my coat. My suitcase and other bags were already out by the main desk. "OK," I yelled, "let's do it!" and I walked out the door and down the hall. The few staff who were around said good-bye, good luck, etc., and I waved and smiled as I passed. Susan opened the wing door for me, and I walked down a short hall into the visiting area where my family was waiting. We entered and my parents were there with Josh, who must have been conscripted for this trip. Josh was parked on a couch with his feet up, face stuck in a Sports Illustrated, and Mom and Dad were pacing around the room. They looked more nervous than me. They all turned as we entered, and Mom and Dad broke out into broad smiles. "Hey, Molly!" Dad said as brightly as possible, and Mom jumped in with "Hi, honey!"

"Hi, Mom, Hi, Dad," I said as they hustled over and took turns giving me enthusiastic hugs. I threw in a "Hi, Josh," just to be polite, and Josh looked up, smiled with passable sincerity, and waved before plunging back into his magazine.

"Is she all ready to go?" Dad asked Susan.

"She is," Susan answered. "She's all set. And she's still scheduled to see Dr. Raimes?"

Mom spoke up. "Yes, Susan, her first appointment is in three days and we've scheduled appointments for the next several weeks in advance just to make sure she's got a spot."

"Great. As I told you before, I'll be in touch with you for awhile to make sure things are going OK, and <u>don't hesitate</u> to call me if I can help. OK?"

"OK," they both answered.

"All right, then. I guess this is it." Susan turned to me. "Molly?"

"Yeah?"

"Can you do something for me?"

"Anything, Susan. You name it."

"Have a good life. You got that? <u>Have a good life</u>. I'll miss you."

"I'll miss you, too." For what was likely the last time, we hugged again. "Good-bye, Susan."

"Good-bye, Molly."

Dad and Mom both came over, took turns shaking her hand, and thanked her profusely. Dad picked up my suitcase and directed Josh to get the other couple of bags, which he did with unusual eagerness. Was it possible that even Josh missed me? Nah! I had to be reading too much into it. Mom opened the door and we traveled down the hall and back into the elevator that had delivered me to this place all those days before. As the elevator door slid closed, I looked one last time down the hall to the Clinic entrance and whispered "good-bye" under my breath. It was weird! I had felt so strange coming here, and now I felt strange leaving it.

As the elevator descended and the floors flew by with an electronic "ding" as we passed each one, I noticed both my parents just smiling at me, and I smiled back.

"You look great," Dad said.

"Yes, Molly, you really do," Mom concurred.

"Thanks," I said, "I feel pretty good."

"Are you nervous about going home?" Mom asked. "Susan said it might be a bit strange for you at first."

"A little."

"Well, don't worry about it. When we get home, you can just crash for awhile until you get your bearings. I'm going to make lunch, and Dad's going to join us."

"You are?" I asked, turning to him with more than mild surprise as he hadn't joined all three of us for anything since the divorce.

"Yeah," he said, "I figured this was a celebration I didn't want to miss. We're all thrilled to have you home, honey."

"What about Cindy? Where's she? Is this all right with her?"

He laughed. "Absolutely. She's thrilled for you, too, Molly. She just figured it would be better if it was just the immediate family. She sends her best."

"Oh, OK," I said. At that point, the elevator stopped at one of the floors and this nurse got on, so our conversation stopped. We rode to the main floor and everyone got off, and we headed for the exit to the parking lot.

"I'm going to take my car over to the house, and I'll meet all of you there," Dad said to us as we stepped outside.

"OK, Steven, we'll see you there," Mom said, and we all loaded up in her car. The ride home was full of small talk and some awkward silences, and I sort of felt like a guest who had been picked up at the bus station to come for a visit, but I guess that's not too surprising after all that had gone on. I looked at the houses and stores and other scenery I had passed thousands of times before, but everything looked a bit odd, a bit different. It was like that feeling you get after coming home from a long vacation, when the old scenes seemed strange, kind of like seeing it for the first time, but it was OK. It was more interesting than scary, and I thought that must be a good sign.

We rounded the corner to our house, pulled into the driveway, and parked. As we all got out and headed into the house, I remembered that I had pondered this very moment many times while in the Clinic, and now here it was. Home. Right there, right in front of me, right now. I checked my emotional pulse, and it was fine. No panic, no shakes. So far, so good. We all walked in, with Josh doing the "guy" thing, carrying the heavy suitcase, and Mom holding the door for me, like I was coming back from having surgery or something. As I entered the hallway and then the kitchen, everything was both just as I remembered it and all together different. I can't really explain what I mean by that, but that's how it felt. We all took off our coats, Josh dropped the bag in the hall, and Mom began picking various stuff that had been left laying around.

"You guys hungry?" she asked as she folded some newspapers for recycling, and we both nodded. "OK, I have some tomato soup and chips, and I'll get us some sandwiches. Molly, do you need anything?"

"No, Mom. I'm just gonna go put my stuff away in my room."

"All right. I'll call you when everything's ready."

I started to head for my room, and just as I was ready to go up the steps, Dad pulled into the driveway, so I waited for him to come in. He walked in without knocking, and that was something I hadn't seen in ages, but it seemed normal. "Hey, how does it feel to be home? Are you doing OK so far? Are you all right?"

I smiled. "That's about the umpteenth time you two have asked me if I'm OK since this morning. I'm fine, believe me," and I tried to say it with gentle sincerity, because that's how I was feeling.

"OK," he said, "I won't ask you any more. At least not today," and he winked.

"<u>Thank</u> you." I went up the stairs and into my room, and looked around. For old times sake, I flopped on my bed with my head on my pillow, and looked up for my old confidant. However, all I saw was a ceiling. Swirled plaster and white paint. No voices, no questions, and no answers. Just a ceiling. I laid there for a while, waiting to see if anything appeared, but then decided it was plain silly to be staring at this inanimate object. Besides, I wasn't tired. I got up and went downstairs again and we all had lunch. I don't remember the sandwiches but I'll never forget the gathering. We talked, we listened, and we laughed, and that hadn't happened in eons.

Later on, after we had eaten and all helped in the cleaning up, Josh said he was going out to hang out with some friends and left. Before he left, though, he said, "It's good to have you home," and lightly punched me on the arm, an unmistakable sign of brotherly affection. He caught me <u>so</u> off guard with that, and I think I blushed.

"Thanks, Josh. It's good to be home."

"Also," he said, "because you were gone for so long, <u>you</u> get all the dishes for the next two weeks!"

I laughed. "No problem, Bro." He waved good-bye to all of us and left. I sat in the kitchen with Mom and Dad, and we talked about this and that, with Dad making more than his required quota of bad jokes that Mom actually laughed at. To be honest, I did, too, but I was trying to be polite.

After awhile, Dad looked at his watch. "Hey, I gotta get going," he said. "Cindy will be looking for some relief with the baby. He's been real cranky lately. We think he's getting some teeth."

"OK, Steven. Thanks for everything," Mom said.

"Hey, it's nothing. It's the <u>least</u> I could do. Not a problem." He turned to me. "Walk me to the door, Molly?"

"Sure, Dad."

He grabbed his coat and we walked to the front door. As he pulled his coat over his shoulders, he looked at me and said, "Molly, I want you to know, things are going to be different. I don't want you to think that this was all for appearances only. I know I haven't been around for you, but I promise I will be from here on." He zipped his coat, turned to me, and gently cupped both of his hands on each side of my face. "You and Josh are as important to me as anything in this world and I intend to work a lot harder to prove that to you both. I know I've been less than super with that. From now on, we're going to spend more time together, someway, somehow. I'd like the both of you to spend some time with me at my place, too, and get to know Cindy better, because she really is a wonderful person. I also want your stepbrother to get to know what wonderful siblings he has. I know you both are teenagers now and have your own lives and friends that you want to be with, but I really believe we can work it out if we try. I've thought a lot about it since, uh, well, since all this stuff happened. What do you think?"

"I think that's good, Daddy."

He smiled, and then sighed. "You know, you haven't called me 'Daddy' since you were a little girl."

"Is that OK with you?"

He wrapped his arms around me and squeezed hard. "That's just fine with me, Molly. That's just fine." He gave me a big kiss, smiled, turned and left. I watched him get into his car and pull away, and I thought it could be nice to actually have a father again. I wasn't naive enough to think it was going to be all sweetness and light, mind you, but he looked like he was trying, and that was a step in the right direction.

The rest of the afternoon passed relatively uneventfully, and that was just fine with me after all that had gone on, and I watched some TV, put my stuff away, and took a shower. It was nice to have a bathroom all to myself. There was some chitchat with Mom and Josh, catching up on recent news, and it felt less strained as time went by. At one point, as I was stretched out on the couch, watching nothing in particular on the tube, the phone rang. I didn't pay much attention but then Mom showed up.

"It's a call for you, Molly," she said.

"OK, Mom. Who is it?" I was wondering why she came to tell me in person, rather than just yodeling it out, as was the family custom.

"It's Craig." Oh, so that's why I was getting personal service. Mom looked at me with concern. "Do you think you're up for this yet? Do you want me to ask him to call back tomorrow or something?"

"How did he know I was home?"

"Are you kidding? He's been checking in on a regular basis. I've spoken to him more since you were gone than when you were home. He must have this house on speed dial. He was getting to be a pest." I was both thrilled and terrified to hear that.

"Why don't you want me to talk to him, then?"

"I didn't say I don't want you to talk to him, Molly. Maybe just not yet. You just got home. I think maybe you should wait a day or so until you get your bearings a bit. I don't want you to get stressed by anything until you've settled in a bit. I want you to relax."

"Mom, I've spent most of my days sitting around just talking. If I was any more relaxed, I'd pass out! I can handle it, Mom! I can! Please?"

I think she was feeling too good about me being home to deny me. "Well, all right, <u>but</u> not for long! And <u>don't</u> make any plans for today. He can see you tomorrow. For a <u>little</u> while. <u>Here</u>."

"Aw, Mom!"

"Take it or leave it."

I sighed, but I knew she was right. "All right, all right. Can I at least talk to him without you hanging around, spying on me?"

"What? <u>Me</u>? You've <u>got</u> to be kidding!"

"<u>Mom</u>!"

"OK, OK, but don't push it. Really, don't stay on too long. Humor me."

"I won't, I promise! Now, will you get lost?"

She smiled and left. I lifted the phone to my ear. "Hello?"

"Hey, Molly, this is Craig. How are you? It's great to hear your voice again."

"I'm good, Craig. I really am. How are you?"

"I'm fine. It's been kinda boring, though. You know, same old, same old. School, homework, and all that garbage. <u>But</u>, I have managed to bug your family calling all the time, asking about you, how you were doing and stuff."

"I'm sure they didn't mind."

"No, they were nice when I called. So, how was it?"

"How was what?"

"That place you were at, the Clinic."

I didn't know yet just how to summarize my time away. That's not to say that I hadn't thought about that when I was there. Heck, I thought about that frequently. But, how does one explain a long lonely walk on the dark side of the moon, along the sharp deep edge of the pit? How do you describe a forced vacation at Camp Crazy? Where do you begin to describe people you grew to know in ways you never knew any one else, and with whom you shared secrets you never shared with anyone else? While we had some discussion about these kinds of return issues at the Clinic before I left, it seemed a whole lot more abstract now that I was here compared to when I was there. "Oh, it was OK." Deep, Molly, <u>really</u> deep!

"And how are you? Are you OK?"

"Yeah, Craig, I'm good, actually. My family is treating me like I barely survived an attack of the Ebola virus or something, but I'm fine."

"Well, I'm <u>really</u> glad you're home. It's been a bit weird. I mean, we were just getting to know each other, and I know we only met that one time, but I actually missed you a lot. Strange, isn't it?"

"Oh, I don't know. I missed you, too. So, if you're strange, then you're not alone."

"I guess that's good news. I think."

"When are you going back to school?"

"Tomorrow."

"So, you're jumping right back into it? I thought you might be home for awhile."

"Doing what? Staring at the walls? I don't think so. I'm supposed to get back into my normal activities, so I'm going back."

"So, is it possible I can see you before you go back?"

"Like tonight? I don't know. Mom's being somewhat motherly, if you know what I mean. Besides, it's Sunday night."

"Oh." He sounded disappointed.

"Maybe," I said, "you can come over here."

"Would that be OK with your Mom?"

"I'm not sure. Let me work on her for awhile. Call me back in about an hour and I'll let you know."

"OK. Hey, whatever she says, I'm happy you're home, and I'm happy you're feeling better. If we can't do anything tonight, we'll get together some other night."

"OK. Thanks for calling. It was good to talk to you."

"Same here. Bye."

"Bye," I said, and we both hung up. I stood there, feeling somewhat amazed, but more relieved. I had certainly spent a fair amount of time wondering if we would be able to pick up where we had left off, and apparently we just might be able to do it. Despite it all, he still was interested, still wanted to see me. I had worried that he would have either lost interest or been spooked away by now, but I sort of kept that worry under wraps when I was in the "big house." Miracles can come true, it can happen to me. I know that doesn't rhyme like the original, but deal with it!

I now faced my first Mom-manipulation since my return, but I was up for it. Heck, this was the new, "can-do" Molly. Ever upward, the sky's the limit, go for the gusto, and all that other happy garbage.

"Hey, Mom?" I said as I strolled into the living room where she was kicking back in a recliner, remote in hand and flipping through the channels.

"Yeah, Molly, what's up?"

"I know you're probably going to say no to this...."

She sat up straight and turned to me with a "What now?" expression. "Probably say no to what?" she asked suspiciously.

"Well, I know you said you didn't want me to really do anything today, you just wanted me to relax but, Mom, I'm so relaxed I can't stand it!"

"And so you want to do what?" She was waiting for the other shoe to drop.

"Well, that was Craig on the phone and..."

"No."

"What do you mean, 'no'? I didn't even ask you anything yet."

"I know exactly what you mean. You want to see him today, don't you?"

"C'mon, Mom! I haven't seen him like <u>forever</u>, and we've only really seen each other once. Can't he just come over for a little while? <u>Please</u>? It won't be long, I promise! What's it going to hurt?"

"I already told you, Molly, I think you had enough stress today just coming home. I want you to just take it easy, and you've got your first day back to school tomorrow. That's going to be stressful enough."

Now, the former Molly would have just ranted and raved for awhile, would have created five more problems than she started with, and would have still wound up with a big fat no. However, the new Molly really did learn a technique or two while away. "Mom, you know they said at the Clinic that it would be good for me to start to talk calmly about my problems and try to work them out, and I think this would be a good time when we can do that."

Mom looked at me suspiciously. "Oh, really? Interesting you should pick this problem to begin with."

"Well, first, we both take turns saying what we think the problem is. Then, we try to come up with a lot of solutions to the problem. After we've got a bunch, we try to decide which one would work best, or give us what they called a 'win-win' solution. And then," I said with a certain air of finality, "we pick one and use it."

Mom smiled. "Oh, <u>this</u> is interesting! So you're now a junior therapist, are you?"

"Hey, Mom, don't joke! You never know. Sometimes, people who've been through a problem can help others with the same kinds of problems the best. Maybe I <u>will</u> be a therapist some day. It's possible. I think I could be good at it."

She smiled. "Somehow, honey, I think you could be, too. If not that, then a used car salesman, or something."

"So, uh, about Craig?"

"OK, then, if we're going to do this, let's do this. Here," she said, while pulling out two kitchen chairs, "have a seat." We both plonked down and Mom put her face in her hands and looked at me. "Go for it," she said.

"All right. Here goes." I cleared my throat for effect. "I think the problem is that I haven't had the chance to talk to anyone outside of the Clinic since I left. I know it's soon, but I don't know what difference it's going to make if I wait for another day or two or three. If I'm supposed to be better, than I'm not sure why I can't do something. I'm only asking for a couple of hours, we'll be right here just watching movies, and you can check on me any time." I stopped for dramatic effect. "So, what do you think?"

"OK," Mom said. "Now what?"

"You tell me what you heard."

"All right. Let's see. You said that you're frustrated because you don't see the reason for waiting, you think you're ready, it's only a couple of hours, and I can check on you if I need to. How's that? How did I do?"

"Not bad for a rookie, Mom. Not bad. Now, you tell me what you think the problem is."

"OK. Here goes. I think the problem for me is that I'm a nervous wreck about you, and that I'm worried that if you talk to or see <u>anybody</u>, that you might get hurt again, and if you get hurt again, you might hurt yourself again, and if you hurt yourself again, I couldn't take it, because the sight of you bleeding....." Her eyes clouded up a bit. "The thought of you...." She gasped a bit and stopped, trying to keep her composure. "Well," she said, "I think you get the picture. I think that, if it was up to me, you'd stay <u>right here</u>," and she pointed to the floor for emphasis, "and I'd keep you sheltered from all the bad things out there." She smiled, and a single big, fat tear rolled down her cheek. "<u>But</u>," she said loudly after taking a deep breath, "I know that's not possible. I know that I've got to let you go, let you go back to the real world. So," she said, "Let me skip ahead to the solution. Craig can come over here <u>but</u> only for a couple of hours. And <u>only</u> here. Deal?"

I managed to keep my smile reasonably subdued. "You know, Mom, for a rookie, you're pretty darn good at this problem-solving stuff," and I lightly punched her on the arm.

"Don't give me that condescending BS," she said. "I could still change my mind."

"Absolutely not," I said, and raised my right arm to a pledging position.

We worked out the particulars about when and where and what, and I kissed mom in gratitude. I ran and called Craig back and told him the good news, and he agreed to come over around 8:00 after he grabbed a movie or two for us to watch. With Mom's help, I checked the snack and soda supply, and then went about primping myself for the night, which felt kind of weird. Oh, sure, I did the basic make-up stuff every day but I never really put a great deal of thought or effort into it. Tonight, though, I was more than a little bit fussy, a little bit particular, and when I was done, I stood back and surveyed my work. "Not bad, Molly, not bad," I said out loud to myself. There might be hope for me yet.

Time crawled, and I worked hard at not staring at the clock, but eventually evening came. Eight o'clock came and went, and then 8:05, and then 8:10. At 8:12, though, the doorbell rang. Mom got up to answer but retreated back to her chair after I blew by her. I opened the door and Craig was there, videotapes in hand.

"Hey, Molly."

"Hi, Craig."

"How are you?"

"I'm good. How are you?"

"Good, I'm good. C'mon in."

He stepped in and we walked into the family room. I took his coat for him and tossed it over a chair and we sat down. There was this brief gap where words were hard to find, and I think neither of us knew where to begin. I mean, we just couldn't pick up where we were. There was too much that had gone on, and he had no real idea what it was

196

all about. Somebody had to bridge the gap and I figured it should be me, as I was the one who created it.

"I guess I owe you some explanation so I'll start this conversation," I said. "I'm sure this all must have been real confusing for you."

"Hey, don't worry about me. But, yes, you might say that. Yeah, a little bit. What happened?"

"Believe me, Craig, it had nothing to do with you. There was a ton of stuff that was going on before we met that screwed me up, and it just got to be too much. I've felt really bad about it, and I figured you'd think I was plain crazy. One day I'm there, and then I'm not. I'm sorry, I didn't mean to mess with your head."

"No, no! Don't feel that way! Heck, I was worried about you. I wish there was something I could have done to help. I was worried that I might have done something, but I couldn't figure out what that could have been. But then I'd think, what is it I could have done? We only knew each other for one night. But then I'd think, I should have seen something, should have done something. I should have noticed that you weren't feeling OK, but you seemed fine to me that night. I felt, y'know, kind of guilty, like I must have missed something, I should have done something."

"Oh, no, Craig, don't think that! Don't! Guilt is my specialty! You were just unlucky enough to be in the wrong place at the wrong time. I was already pretty far over the edge by that time. There wasn't anything you could have done. Please, I don't want you to take any responsibility for my problems. They were there a long time before you."

"Still..."

"No! There is no 'still.' This was my baggage. Mine! In fact, you were one of my positive memories while I was there."

"Really?"

"Yes, really."

"That's good to hear, Molly. I was worried."

197

"Well, stop worrying, OK?"

"OK. Hey, we don't have to talk about it if you don't want to."

"Actually, talking is one of the things I learned how to do better when I was at the Clinic, and I sure got a lot more practice doing it."

"Is that a good thing?"

"Yes," I said, smiling. "It's a good thing."

"So do you want to?"

"Want to what?"

"Talk about it."

"Oh, yeah, sure. C'mon, I'm going to be asked about it enough when I go back to school, anyway. I might as well practice now. Where do you want to start? What do you want to know?"

"Well, how about why?"

"Why? Oh, why don't you start with a hard question, huh?" He smiled. "OK, then." I sighed. "It's not like there was any one thing, you know, it was a lot of things. It's not like you see in the movies where some big thing happens that pushes you over the edge, like somebody dies or something. I think I'd been unhappy for a long time, and I didn't even realize it, or didn't realize how much. You know, you can find out that you've been walking around and going through the motions, like waking up, going to school, coming home, going to bed, and doing all the usual stuff, but something's not right. I got so used to feeling shitty that it started to seem normal. I sort of assumed that most everybody felt that way."

"That sounds like it sucks!"

"Yeah, it does."

"Was it like problems with your family, or school, or what?"

"Oh, it was family stuff, for sure, and school stuff, too. But, you know, I also I found out it's about me, too. There were kids there who talked about their lives and they seemed pretty good. They couldn't come up with anything that was way out of whack, they just felt shitty. Others? Well, they had some bad stuff going on, so it was easier to see why. We also talked about other people we knew whose lives were worse than ours who were doing fine. So, part of it is me, and how I choose to look at things. You know, it is what it is. Sometimes, I can't change that, but maybe I can change the way I look at it."

"Woah, that's some deep stuff."

I smiled. "Hey, you asked!"

"So, you're all better?"

"Uh, no <u>way</u>! I just have a better idea of what the problem is. That alone was a <u>big</u> improvement. My family also was really great. I sort of assumed that they didn't give a shit, but they really surprised me. My Mom and Dad really seemed to try, and that was a major surprise for me. It seemed like we were able to talk about stuff that hadn't been talked about for like forever, and that helped a lot. I just hope we'll be able to keep it up. That has me a little nervous, to tell you the truth. I mean, I'm optimistic and everything, but it's easy to talk deep and talk honest when you're sitting there in these intense therapy sessions. They kind of have you trapped. I just hope we can keep it up now that I'm back.."

"So, do you go back there for any more help, or anything? Are you done there?"

"Oh, I'm done there, but I'm not done. Actually, I'm set up to see this psychologist I started with here just before I left. He was a nice guy, and I think that'll help. My family will be coming, too, when I need it. Everybody agreed to do that, so that's good. The way I am, I'll probably be in therapy forever!"

"Hey," he said with this real encouraging tone, "that's OK, if it helps. That's OK."

"I'm fine with that, don't get me wrong. It sure beats where I was. I'll go as long as I need it."

"How about school? What was up with that?"

"It's not like I don't have friends or anything, because I do. I just never thought anybody would be interested in my stuff, and I felt guilty about bothering them with my stuff. Actually," I said, "I learned that I <u>gotta</u> stop feeling so guilty. I was blaming myself for <u>everything</u>! I think global warming was the only thing I wasn't beating myself up for." He laughed.

"So, you think you're ready to go back to school tomorrow?"

"I think so. I hope so. What else am I gonna do? I can't just hang out here. My counselor told me I've got to work on my relationships, and she even had me practice doing it when I was there. I am <u>really</u> nervous, though, really nervous."

"I'm sure you'll be fine. You'll do good. You really sound like you know what you're talking about."

"Talk is cheap."

"Hey, c'mon, don't worry about it! You've got friends. I'll be there for you. It'll be all right," and he took my hand in his. He smiled at me with this big encouraging smile, and I leaned over and kissed him.

"Thanks," I said. "I needed that." We spent the rest of the evening just cuddling and watching the tube, and it was real nice. Mom was discreet but there, and after a couple of hours she made her self more obvious, looking at me and then her watch. I got the hint..

"Craig?"

"Don't tell me, let me guess. I gotta go?"

"So, you got the vibes, too? Hey, Mom was being generous as it was. I don't want to push it."

"Believe me, I don't want you to push it, either. I've been annoying enough as it is with my phone calls. Besides," he said, "you're home now. With a little luck, we might do this again?"

"Yes, I am home. And I plan on staying around for awhile. I've done enough traveling for the time being."

He stood up, reached out his hand for mine, and gently pulled me up. Together, we walked towards the door and when we arrived, I opened it for him, and we both stepped outside into the cold night. Despite the temperature, I closed the door behind me, as I didn't want my "bodyguard" snooping on me just now. "Can I kiss you good-bye?" Craig asked.

"You better."

We kissed, and I squeezed him hard. There was a feeling with this embrace that meant so much to me. To me, it meant a happy ending to a very unhappy story. It meant that I must be worth something if someone would hold with me through this. It meant a beginning of what would be my new life, sort of like a rebirth, because I really felt I had excised a lot of the demons who had possessed me for so long a time. Oh, I knew the past would remain a part of me, and I realized it was important to not forget what I had been through, because I now believed the old saying about how that which does not kill you can make you stronger. However, I also wasn't going to carry the pain anymore. I wasn't. I didn't need to. Good-bye! Good riddance!

Gradually, I lessened my grip on Craig, and we looked at each other. "Molly," he said, "I'm sure you've been through a whole lot that I don't know anything about, and I've got to believe that it isn't easy stuff to talk about. I just want you to know that if you need to, I'm ready to listen. Don't get me wrong, it was fantastic to just be with you tonight. We could have stared at the wall and that would have been just <u>fine</u> with me. Just remember, though, I'm here for you."

"I know we're still just getting to know each other, Craig," I said, "but I can't tell you just how much it meant to me that you stood by me when I was away, and how much it means that you're here now. I'm a bit talked out from the Clinic, and it was great to just be there with you tonight. One of the big things I learned when I was away, though, was to listen to my feelings, and my feelings need some time."

"That's cool with me. I'll give them all the time they need," he said.

"Thank you," I told him with one last hug.

"Ain't nothin'. You're welcome." He gave me a parting quick kiss, turned, and left. I watched him get in his car, start it up, and pull away. As drove up the street, he beeped the horn and waved, and I waved back. I had no idea what was going to happen with Craig when I was away, and I was happy and relieved to find out he was still interested. Again, I was seeing possibilities, and I thought I might have potential if that trend continued.

Back inside, I talked to Mom a little bit, and she was good about not overdoing the questions. I don't think I was the only one who learned something through all this. I gave her a kiss good night and went up to my room to go to bed, as I was pretty beat. OK, mind you, but still beat.

As I lay in bed, I thought about the week ahead. I thought about going back to school next week, and I knew there would be some awkwardness, a million questions asked and a few million more that would never be asked. I felt ready, though. I felt ready. Or at least I thought I was. I held up my arm in the dim light coming from under my bedroom door and looked at some of the fading scars from my cutting, some of which would eventually disappear, and others that were going to be there for the rest of my life. God knows I wasn't thrilled about permanent, lifetime scars, but I thought I could use them to my advantage. I mean, I could look at them and remember how bottling things up <u>didn't</u> work. I could remember just how shitty one can feel if one doesn't try to understand the pain, to look at the pain, to talk back to the pain. I could remember how <u>stupid</u> one can be with this stuff. I knew I was on the "one-day-at-a-time" plan, and today, I was OK. Tomorrow? Tomorrow I started school again. I was a bit freaked about that, but one day at a time, one day at a time.

CHAPTER 13

The alarm clock rang, I opened my eyes, and thought to myself, "OK, I can do this." I don't know how convinced I was, but I was trying. Phony enthusiasm was better than no enthusiasm at all. I figured I could try to talk tough even though I was way nervous. If I didn't go after it, I wasn't going to be able to do it. I got dressed, came downstairs, and grabbed a bowl and some cereal.

"So you're up?" Mom asked with an anxious expression.

"Hey, I'm not only up, I'm ready, and I'm ready before Josh, aren't I?"

"That's not exactly hard now, is it?"

"I can do this, Mom. I can do this. At least, that's what I keep telling myself."

"Don't worry. I've already spoken to the principal about you coming back today and..."

"Mom!"

"Hey, look, Molly, you're not going back in there without some supports, at least until you've settled back in. We're not going to act like you were just on some vacation, or something. This time, we're not going to be naive about this. They've had some communication with the Clinic so they're prepared. Look at it this way; they might be able to keep everybody from asking you the same questions over and over. People are bound to be curious. If you feel stressed or upset, or you feel like you need any kind of help, you can just go to Guidance."

"Mom, I don't want to be treated like some kind of freaking head-case! I just want to go to school like everybody else."

"Look, for most kids, it doesn't mean anything. They're interested in their own lives. They probably didn't even know you were gone, and those that do know you are excited for you. Just relax. By the end of the day it'll probably feel like you never left."

"I hope you're right."

Mom walked over and sat beside me at the table. "Molly, I won't lie to you. I'm nervous, too. But I believe in you. I know you can do this."

"Funny you should put it that way. That's what I've been telling myself since I got up."

"Well, then, let's do it!"

"OK, I'm ready. I think." Mom reached out her palm for a high-five, which I returned with all the gusto I manage. I was trying.

I finished eating and got all my stuff together, most of which I had nervously prepared last night. Mom was driving me in for this first day, so we both got in the car and she drove me to the school. It looked the same when we pulled in front, with some kids walking, some getting out of cars, and others stepping off school buses. Despite all my "positive self-talk," I was a nervous wreck! I grabbed my back pack and Mom said, "Have a good day, dear."

"If I don't throw up first!" I shot back.

"C'mon, Molly, it'll be fine."

"OK, Mom," and I reached over, gave her a kiss, and then stepped out of the car. She beeped and waved. I waved back and turned and walked towards the front door as she pulled away.

As I was opening the front door, I heard a familiar voice call out, "Hey, Molly!" I turned and saw Rebecca waving at me, and I waved back. "Wait up," she yelled, so I closed the door and paused until she caught up. She ran up the steps, dropped her bag, and grabbed me with a big hug. "It's GREAT to see you! How are you?"

"I'm good," I said. "I'm good."

"You look great! We were all thrilled to hear you were coming back. We missed you!"

"I missed you guys, too." We talked as we walked, or rather I should say that she talked and I listened, and she seemed really psyched, which made me feel good. We went to our lockers, and various kids called out with hellos, how ya doings, and what not. Some kids came over and chatted briefly as we made our way to homeroom. As predicted, though, most kids didn't seem to take much notice at all, and that was actually a big relief. After a little while, I just felt like another kid in the school, which is just what I wanted to feel.

I made it through the morning and my teachers all said hi, but they managed to do it in a sort of quiet, private way. They also let me know that they'd help me with whatever I'd missed in school work, which was also a relief because I was a little worried about that.

Lunch time came, and I joined the Lost Lunch Quintet for the first time since I was gone. They all made a fuss over me, which was nice, and Jasmine even produced a small cake she had made for me. "This is for you, Molly," she said warmly. "Welcome back. We missed you." They even gave me a small round of applause as she handed it to me, and it was a little embarrassing but it felt really nice. In some way I was relieved, because I really had no idea how they would react to everything that had gone on. Heck, I didn't know how I was going to react, but their enthusiasm overcame my awkwardness. It's nice to have friends.

"How was it?" Suzanne asked. Everyone else looked at me, and it seemed that Suzanne asked the question they all wanted to know, as they had this look of anticipation.

"It was OK," I said. "It really was."

"Are you doing all right?" Jennifer inquired.

"Yeah," Jasmine continued. "Are you feeling better?"

"I think so. So far, so good."

Suzanne continued, "Do you mind us asking you about it?"

"No, it's fine. I don't mind. What do you want to know?"

There was this long pause, and they all kind of looked at each other before Jennifer said, "Actually, we have no idea!" and everyone cracked up.

"Well, if you get any questions, I don't mind. At least I don't think I will. If I do, how about if I just let you know?"

"That sounds good."

"Yeah, that's a good idea," and then no one asked me anything. I suspect they just needed to know that it was not a taboo subject, and it seemed like once they did it was no big deal. The rest of the day went relatively uneventfully. There were some strange looks from some kids, but they tended to be brief. It generally seemed that most kids didn't have much of an opinion one way or the other, and that was fine with me. Mr. Quinn called me into his office for a few minutes after lunch, and made it clear that he was available if I needed to talk. He said he wasn't trying to take the place of Dr. Raimes, and he was aware of the fact that I'd be in therapy with him. He just wanted me to know that he was there for me, and he wanted to help in any way he could. It was nice, and I appreciated it.

I survived my first day back. By the end of the day, I didn't feel as uncomfortable, and it went a little easier than I had thought it would, although I had no way of knowing what to expect. I mean, I'd never been in this position before. Come to think of it, I didn't know anyone else who had been in this position, either, although we had discussed it in an abstract way at the Clinic. It turned out to be no really big deal, but I'd be lying to you if I said I wasn't relieved. I was. But I did it, and the first day back was over. I took the bus home, which was my deal with Mom, and as I sat looking out the window, I thought to myself, it wasn't so bad. And then I thought, I'm going to make that my new motto - "It's not so bad." That could come in handy in other situations.

And so, here I am, back at home, writing again. I'm not going to kid you, I told you right from the start that life is confusing, and I <u>still</u> think it is. Heck, I think I'd worry about someone who could think it wasn't. And I'm still worried about the future, and how it will turn out, and what it has in store for me. I'm not really what you could call confident yet, and I'm not even sure that I'll ever be able to do that. However, I'm not afraid. I'm not terrified. I don't have that feeling of despair that had brought me to that awful place where drawing my own blood seemed like a positive choice, a better choice than living with the pain. I think that once you've been to that place, it's hard to shake the fear that you might some day find yourself there again, and that's a place I never, ever, want to be again. I hope that fear will diminish as time goes by, but I can only take it a day at a time. Just a day at a time. And so far, this day was a decent one. Tomorrow? We'll see.

I'm going to stop writing now, at least about this. I hope that this story is over. Oh, I know I'll be writing about other stuff, because writing has become as much a part of me as talking, in some ways a more effective medium because I can think about it before it comes out, and then go back and look at it after it's on paper, and if I don't like it, I can cross it out and start all over again, change it. You can't do that when you talk. With that, after it's out, there's no taking it back. It's out there for everyone to hear and react to. Writing, you see, is safer for me. You can interpret this one for what it's worth, get out of it what you can, if anything. But, maybe next time, the story I write will be an all together different one. Maybe I'll write about something like a love story. Yeah, that's the ticket, a love story. Staring yours truly, and maybe this kid named Craig. We'll see.

Bye for now.

About the Author

Dr. Jody Dempsey, Ph.D., is a Clinical Psychologist in Vestal, N.Y. whose clinical practice is devoted to the treatment of troubled children and adolescents and their families. In his twenty year career, Dr. Dempsey has also served as a consultant to numerous schools and agencies treating children and has taught a number of subjects regarding children/family issues at the undergraduate and graduate level at several colleges, including Binghamton University, and has published research in children's issues as well. Most recently, Dr. Dempsey devised, created, and taught a course entitled *Children and Violence* at Binghamton University. He has also written for the media regarding children and nonviolence, and has been interviewed numerous times by area television news stations regarding a variety of children's issues. Dr. Dempsey, aided by a staff of teen volunteers, has conducted a "Peace Camp" teaching nonviolent problem-solving and diversity to hundreds of children for the past nine years. He has also served as a consultant with the Johnson City School District in New York to devise and implement interventions teaching and promoting nonviolence. He is a licensed psychologist in both New York and Pennsylvania, is certified as a School Psychologist, and is a Member of the American Psychological Association and its Divisions of Clinical Child Psychology, Peace Psychology, School Psychology, and Clinical Hypnosis. Dr. Dempsey lives in Vestal with his wife and three sons.